OVER

CONQUER

'More than conquerors . . .'
Unlocking truths to live wisely and well

DEREK STRINGER

British Library Cataloguing In Publication Data
A Record of this Publication is available
from the British Library

ISBN 978-1-84685-691-4

First Published 2007 by
Good News Broadcasting
In association with Exposure Publishing,
an imprint of
Diggory Press Ltd
Three Rivers, Minions, Liskeard, Cornwall, PL14 5LE, UK
and of Diggory Press, Inc.,
Goodyear, Arizona, 85338, USA
WWW.DIGGORYPRESS.COM

Going Where We Can't Go . . .

About sixty percent of the world's people groups have no scriptures at all, but they can understand the spoken word. How do you reach these people? Radio! It goes behind the barriers into places where we can't go. It proclaims the message millions can't or won't read. That's why Good News Broadcasting promotes radio as a way to reach the world. We have seventy committed Bible teachers writing, recording and producing original material in twenty-five languages, representing outreach to a potential audience of over half the world's population.

Dr. Derek Stringer is the radio 'voice' of Good News Broadcasting to the English speaking world with broadcasts on every continent. He brings the words of the Bible alive, making them relevant to our lives, as indeed they are.

Conquering . . .

Part One is based upon a programme series which took as their central theme Romans 8:37: "In all these things we are more than conquerors." There was a tremendous response when these programmes were broadcast. One listener commented, "Understandable talks filled with the Holy Spirit." There are times when we feel anything but over conquerors and here are insights to help.

Combating . . .

Part Two recognises that worry and anxiety are never completely conquered but need to be combated. Here are tried and tested biblical principles. Both sections conclude with a chapter about fear of the future, because this is something to be conquered but constantly combated.

May God bless you as you discover the meaning of being an OVER CONQUEROR.

If you haven't heard any programmes produced by the Good News Broadcasting Association, Please contact us to find out how you can hear them where you are.

You can contact us by writing to:
GNB   Back Lane   Ranskill   Nottinghamshire   DN22 8NN
England
Website: www.gnba.net Email: info@gnba.net

INDEX

PART ONE
CONQUERING...

PART TWO
COMBATING...

PART ONE

CONQUERING…

Chapter 1
Conquering Insecurity

An incident took place in America back in 1887 in a small neighbourhood grocery store when a middle-aged gentleman, Emanuel Nenger, gave the assistant a $20 note to pay for the turnips he was purchasing. When the assistant placed the note in the cash drawer she noticed that some of the ink from the $20 came off on her hands which were wet from wrapping the turnips.

She'd known Mr. Nenger for years and was shocked. She pondered, "Is this man giving me a counterfeit $20 note?" She dismissed the thought immediately and gave him his change. But $20 was a lot of money in those days so she notified the police who, after procuring a search warrant, went to Emanuel Nenger's home where they found, in his attic, the tools he was using to reproduce the counterfeit $20 notes. They found an artist's easel, paint brushes, and paints which Nenger was using to meticulously paint the counterfeit money. He was a master artist.

The police also found three portraits that Nenger had painted - paintings that sold at public auction for a little over $16,000! The irony was that it took him almost as much time to paint a $20 note as it did to paint those portraits which he sold for more than $5,000 each.

Isn't it amazing that he would waste his time doing something so foolish when he had the opportunity to do something so valuable. But we're all guilty of the same thing. Think for a moment about how you spent your time yesterday, or last week. Think of the hours wasted doing things that were unimportant, or maybe even destructive - time which could have been spent developing your relationship with God and helping others.

God gives each one of us the gift of 1,440 minutes every day. In terms of time, no one is any richer than anyone else.

We all get exactly the same amount. Like the manna given to the Hebrews in the wilderness, none of those minutes can be stored up and used the next day, they must be used on the day they were given. But how we use those minutes is our choice. We need to choose wisely. As the apostle Paul put it, "Be careful then how you live, not as unwise people but as wise, making the most of the time, because the days are evil."

How we live our lives is very important.

Romans 8 has been called 'The high point in the New Testament.' It certainly has insights to help us live the Christian life effectively. The Greek word for 'spirit' occurs thirty-four times in the book of Romans and twenty-one of these are to be found in this chapter. In only two of the twenty-one references does the term clearly refer to something other than the Holy Spirit. Chapter 8 is supremely the chapter of the Spirit.

In Romans 8 Paul presents his doctrine of the Holy Spirit; yet his purpose at this point isn't to tell us about the person of the Holy Spirit. It's rather to spell out the role of the Spirit in His relationship to our lives as believers. In the first half of the chapter we have *Life In The Spirit*. In the second half, from verse 18, we have the *Triumph Of Believing*. The entire chapter is built around the work of the Spirit.

To grasp Paul's teaching on the Spirit is to understand the secret of living victoriously while surrounded by pressures and problems. How to live in and by the Spirit is the single most important lesson the believer can ever learn.

Paul would be the last person in the world to say that once you become a Christian all your problems will be over. On one occasion he listed some of the trials he had to put up with. The list includes prison, flogging, repeated exposure to death, shipwrecks, dangers. The walk of faith is no bed of roses. Sharing in the suffering of Christ, as Paul called it, is a necessary prelude to sharing in His glory.

10

Thinking about the Gospel of Christ and the benefits of believing; that is, our sins forgiven and a Saviour to live in our lives to do things through us - Paul asks a rhetorical question in verse 31: *"What, then, shall we say in response to this? If God is for us, who can be against us?"* God's provision leaves us speechless! With God on our side it couldn't matter less who might be against us. Like a small boy in the company of an older brother we walk through life unconcerned about opposition that would terrify us if we were alone. God for us is the heart of the Good News.

Verse 32 indicates exactly HOW God is for us. "He did not spare his own Son, but gave him up for us all..." Paul uses the word that God spoke to Abraham on the occasion of the sacrifice of Isaac. As Abraham was willing to give his son in loyal obedience to divine command, so also God sacrificed His Son on our behalf.

But God is also for us in that, along with the gift of His Son, He *"graciously gives us all things"*. God lavishes upon us in sheer extravagance all that He has to give. In Christ, we become heirs to every spiritual blessing. We are the most highly favoured of all mankind.

Paul triumphantly asks, *"Who shall separate us from the love of Christ?"* Can anything drive a wedge between the Christian and his Lord? He quotes from Psalm 44 to remind us that the people of God have always faced tribulation and extreme privation: *"For your sake we face death all day long; we are considered as sheep to be slaughtered."* But we are reminded that: *"... in all these things we are more than conquerors through him who loved us."*

Because we've experienced the transforming power of the love of God not only can we conquer the problems and setbacks of life but we can 'over-conquer', that is we can take the obstacle and use it as a stepping stone. That which was meant to defeat becomes the instrument of our victory. This is what it means to *'more than conquer'*.

Paul's final words in Romans 8, verses 38 and 39 need to be read carefully to allow God's Spirit to bring home the full impact. *"For I am convinced that neither death nor life, neither angels nor demons, neither the present nor the future, nor any powers, neither height nor depth, nor anything else in all creation, will be able to separate us from the love of God that is in Christ Jesus our Lord."*

The danger and poison of insecurity.

We do live in dangerous and difficult times. If we feel insecure, it's because we are insecure. The world never was as safe as we thought it was. No wonder we all feel a bit more anxious these days. Researchers say there are five primary marks of insecurity: Helplessness, isolation, vulnerability, fear of the future, and extreme pessimism. Insecurity leads us to say things like this: "Something bad is going to happen and there's nothing I can do about it. And no one can help me." Often it's not the "big picture" that troubles us as much as the problems of daily life. We worry about our finances, our job security, whether or not our marriage will make it, our health, what will happen in our old age, our investments, and a whole host of personal issues that sap our courage and cause us to stay awake at night worrying about tomorrow, or the day after tomorrow or next week, or next month, or next year.

I believe the biblical answer to insecurity is found in the doctrine of God's *providence*. In English the word "providence" has two parts. It's 'pro' and 'video' put together, literally meaning "to see before". Though the word *providence* is not found in most modern translations of the Bible, the concept is certainly biblical. It refers to "God's gracious oversight of the universe". Every one of those words is important. God's providence is one aspect of his grace. Oversight means that he directs the course of our affairs. The word universe tells us that God not only knows the big picture, he also concerns himself with the tiniest details.

Here are five statements that unfold the meaning of God's providence in more detail:

He upholds all things.
He governs all events.
He directs everything to its appointed end.
He does this all the time and in every circumstance.
He does it always for His own glory.

As R.C. Sproul said, "God doesn't roll dice." Nothing ever happens by chance.

When Jesus was giving instructions to his disciples in Matthew 10, he repeatedly warned them that they were going out to minister to a hostile world. Even though some people would oppose them and try to put them to death, they should not be afraid of what might happen to them. Dropped in the middle of this sober message is a passage that contains the grounds for security in a very insecure world. Where can we go for safety when there is so much trouble in the world?

Let's see how Jesus answers the question, "Are not two sparrows sold for a penny? Yet not one of them will fall to the ground apart from the will of your Father." Sparrows were among the humblest birds in Bible times. They were considered food for the poor, and because they were so cheap, the poor could offer them in sacrifice to the Lord if they couldn't afford a lamb or a goat or a bull. You could buy two sparrows for a penny. That's pretty cheap by any standard. You could feed your family sparrow casserole very cheaply.

I used to think that Jesus was saying that God watches the sparrows when they fall. I suppose I've heard that wonderful song Ethel Waters made famous so many times that it sticks in my mind: *"His eye is on the sparrow and I know he watches me."* True enough, he does see the sparrow when it falls. But this verse is saying much more than that. Not only does God see the sparrow when it falls, the sparrow cannot and will not fall apart from the Father's will. The mention of the word "Father" makes it very tender and very personal. It's not as if sparrows fall at random from the trees and God takes note when it happens. The sparrow falls because God willed it to fall, and if he didn't, the sparrow

13

would never fall to the ground. This is a high view of God's involvement in the tiny and seemingly insignificant details of the universe.

Note two implications of this truth:

1) The sparrows do fall.
Even the little sparrows fall to the ground eventually. Sooner or later troubles do come to all of God's children. Sometimes we fall into the romantic notion that coming to Christ will solve all our problems so that we will be free from trouble and sadness. Not so. He makes his rain to fall on the just and the unjust. What happens to people of the world happens to us too. They get sick, we get sick. They lose their jobs, we lose our jobs. They have family problems, we have family problems. They get ripped off, we get ripped off. They get cancer, we get cancer. They die, we die. It is the same for us as for everyone else. Though we know the Lord, we are not exempt from any of the trials and troubles of this world.

2) The sparrows fall according to the Father's will.
As the great confessions tell us, all things take place according to the counsel and decree of Almighty God. There is a very real sense in which everything in the universe must fit into God's ultimate plan somehow.

Even the falling of the sparrow is part of God's providential oversight of the universe. This applies to our pain, our suffering, our loss, and it applies to the heartache of watching our loved ones suffer.

"And even the very hairs of your head are all numbered" said Jesus. Have you ever tried to count the number of hairs on your head? Most of us probably tried that when we were children, but we learned quickly that it was a futile exercise. Not surprising really, the average human head is covered with 100,000 strands of hair. 50 strands fall out each day no matter what we do. Interestingly, the amount of hair varies by colour. Blondes have an average of 140,000 strands of hair, brunettes 105,000, and redheads 90,000.

This is fascinating trivia but it's not something I think about often, and when I do think about my hair, it's always in the aggregate: Is it too long, too short, and not enough of it? Is it combed properly? I never pick out a strand of hair and say to myself, "I wonder how Number 437 is doing?" I don't number the hairs on my head but God does. Our God is a God of the details. He numbers all the hairs on my head. Think about that for a moment. Millions and billions of hairs. He numbers them all. The meaning of this is clear: if God cares for things that matter so little, then he cares for things that matter much more. If God knows each strand of hair individually, he knows each of us individually as well. This means that God's knowledge of us is not just general but amazingly specific. He knows us through and through and he knows us in minute detail. In fact, he knows us far better than we know ourselves.

In a sermon on this verse called *"Providence,"* Charles Spurgeon illustrates God's minute care from the life of Joseph in Genesis. He points out that there was a "chain of circumstances" that had to happen in a particular way in order for the story to take place as it did. Spurgeon offers a long series of questions –

> Why did Jacob want to send Joseph?
> Why were Joseph's brothers on this particular day in a different location?
> Why did the Ishmaelites come along at that moment?
> Why were they in the mood to purchase a slave?
> Why were they going to Egypt and not to some other destination?
> Why did Potiphar purchase Joseph?
> Why did his wife have designs on Joseph?
> Why were the baker and cup bearer in the prison when Joseph was there?
> Why couldn't Pharaoh remember his dream?
> Why did the cup bearer remember Joseph?

Spurgeon points out that every single one of these seemingly unconnected events had to happen in a particular way at a particular time in order for Joseph to be in the right place at the right time to preserve his family in Egypt during the great famine in Canaan. Spurgeon goes on to say that "God is to be seen in little things". He uses a lovely phrase to describe all those "random" details. They are the "minutiae of Providence."

Here is the end of the matter. You are worth more than the sparrows. "Two for a penny!" Tiny sparrows, worth so little, and yet God cares for each one of them. But you are worth more than a bushel of sparrows. How do I know this? Because Jesus didn't die for the sparrows. He died for you and for me. His blood is the badge of his love, the proof of his everlasting affection.

The impact and wonder of Divine providence

First, it should give us boldness in the time of trouble. If God is for us, and He is, why should we fear anything or anyone?

Second, it should give us confidence in the moment of confusion. Today many things are unclear, uncertain and undecided. We all have many more questions than we have answers. So much of life seems like stumbling through the deep fog of hazardous circumstances. Keep moving forward. Things that are unclear now will be made clear in the end. Our God will make all things plain and all his ways will be proved right.

Third, it should give us hope in the time of sorrow. Oh, we weep, all of us weep, the tears flow behind closed doors and in the private moments of life. When we face death, how can we not weep for loved ones who have left us? But be of good cheer. Even death itself is in God's hands. If you are a Christian, you cannot die before God's appointed time. A Christian is immortal until his work on earth is done. Why should we shake? Why should we fear? Let the world shake and fear. It is for us to be calm when others are giving way to fear.

Let me quote directly from Spurgeon: "Especially may I address this remark to timid people. There are some of you

who are frightened at every little thing. Oh! If you
believe that God manages all, why, you would
screaming because your husband is not home when the
a little thunder and lightning, or because there is a mouse
the parlour, or because there is a great tree blown down in
the garden."

So now we come to the bottom line. Do you believe God
ordains all things according to his own will? Some people -
many people, I'm sure - struggle at this very point. We like
to talk about "free will" more than God's ordination of all
things in the universe. But while I truly and deeply believe in
free moral choices for which we will all be held accountable,
in the end I think we must say what the Bible says, that "all
things" work together as part of God's unfolding plan of
redemption. If this is so, then there is no such thing as luck
or fate or chance or happenstance. Everything is either
caused by God or allowed by God, and there is no third
category. The Bible teaches it. Do you believe this? I know I
do.

Let this great truth be the source of your security. Rest in
the Lord. Lay your soul upon the solid rock of God's eternal
providence. Rest in his control over all things. Rest there,
and you will sleep well.

Trusting Divine providence.

But, someone might say, "What about the troubles that may
come tomorrow?" The answer is simple. Either they will not
come, or they will come and some good from God will come
with them. That "good" will not always be seen immediately
or easily, but it is always there because our God uses all
things, wastes nothing, and intends for us only that which is
for our good and His ultimate glory. Thus I conclude that
God's providence is the answer to all insecurity.

In 1871 a great fire destroyed much of the city of Chicago.
Three hundred people died and one hundred thousand were
left homeless. A Chicago lawyer named Horatio Spafford
lost part of his fortune in the fire. He was a Christian and an

great evangelist D. L. Moody. After
years rebuilding his fortune and helping
erything in the fire, Mr. Spafford resolved
nd four children to England where they
Mr. Moody and Mr. Sankey on their
des. Later he planned to move the family
Jerusalem. After purchasing tickets on a
luxury liner due to set sail in November 1873, Mr. Spafford
was unable to go at the last moment because of unfinished
business in Chicago.

He instructed his wife Anna and their four children, Maggie,
Tanetta, Annie, and Bessie, to go on ahead and he would
cross the Atlantic on a later voyage and meet them in
England. On November 22 an English freighter struck the
luxury liner, causing it to sink in only twelve minutes.
Hundreds were lost and only forty-seven survivors were
pulled from the icy waters. In the chaos all four of the
Spafford daughters drowned. Rescuers found Anna
Spafford unconscious and clinging to a piece of wreckage.
She and the other survivors were taken to Cardiff, Wales.
From there she cabled the awful news to her husband in
America. The telegram contained two words: "Saved alone."
Broken-hearted, Mr. Spafford purchased a ticket on the next
ship leaving New York. At one point the captain called Mr.
Spafford to his post and told him that according to the
charts, the ship was passing over the spot where his
daughters had drowned. Overwhelmed with sorrow as he
paced the deck, the words of Isaiah 66:12 were ringing in
his mind, "I will extend peace to her like a river."

Going back to his cabin, he composed the words to a poem
that has become a beloved hymn we still sing today:
When peace, like a river, attendeth my way,
When sorrows, like sea-billows, roll;
Whatever my lot, Thou hast taught me to say,
It is well, it is well, with my soul.
Though Satan should buffet, though trials should come,
Let this blest assurance control,
That Christ hath regarded my helpless estate,
And hath shed His own blood for my soul.

No doubt thinking of the day when he would be reunited with his daughters, he penned the final verse:
And Lord, haste the day when my faith shall be sight,
The clouds be rolled back as a scroll;
The trump shall resound, and the Lord shall descend,
Even so, it is well with my soul.

These are the words of a man who has discovered the solid rock of God's providence. Having lost his four daughters, he has not lost his faith in God. All is well because God is in control of all things, even the hardest tragedies of life. This truth does not remove the pain but it makes a way for us to *keep believing* even while our hearts are breaking.

May God give us this same faith so that when all earthly hope is lost, we may still say, "It is well, it is well with my soul."

Chapter 2
Conquering Disappointment

"I thought everything was fine with my parents", she wrote. "Then, one evening as my sister and I were watching TV, my mum came downstairs to tell us we had to talk. I though it was something good, so I was happy and excited. But instead my mum and dad told us they were having problems, and my mum, sister and I were going to live in a flat. So we moved. It's almost been a year since they have been separated. To top it all off, my mum wants a divorce now. I feel so bad. It's not fair. My mum lies to me and who knows what else she does? I'm mad at her. I feel like she is sneaking around and doing stuff she isn't supposed to do. But", this young writer concludes, "I can't do anything about it. It'll happen even if I don't want it to happen. If I try to change things, someone might get mad."

What you've just read is an excerpt from a school-girl's essay reproduced with permission from her and her mum. You can just sense the overwhelming disappointment in every line. You know what she titled her assignment? "The Big Shock."

That's a good way to describe some of the disappointments that you and I face. They come to us seemingly out of nowhere. Big shocks - sudden, traumatic, and devastating. Dashed hopes and dreams, like those of this young girl; rejection by a friend or a spouse; loss of a job; death of a loved one.

Maybe you've experienced a few "big shock" disappointments in your life. Maybe you're going through one right now.

Romans 8:37 says, "In all things we are more than conquerors through Him who loved us." That's a verse that powerfully sums up what Jesus Christ can do for us. Our Gospel is one of being forgiven and ready for eternity because He died to take away our guilt before a Holy God.

But He also rose from the dead, ascended and by the power of the Holy Spirit comes to live inside each one of us. Christianity is not just about the saving death of Christ. It's also the saving life of Christ. His life in our life helping us to handle the pressures and problems.

When Paul writes about us being 'more than conquerors' the word literally means 'over conqueror'.

The nature of disappointment.

Some disappointments aren't big shocks, they're more like "emotional arthritis", chronic, ongoing, persistent, and seemingly designed to wear down our spirits over time. Loneliness; injustice; the difficult circumstance - such as a physical or emotional illness - that's never going to change. And then there are the nagging disappointments of daily living. The car breaks down. You pull a muscle playing ball. The vacation gets cancelled because the children are sick. This is the level of adversity on which most of us live everyday.

But no matter what level we're on, the question is: How can we deal with the disappointment? How can we find some sense of peace and comfort, whether the disappointment we face is shock-level, "emotional arthritis"-level or nag-level?

Let me start out by sharing a few observations I've made over the last few years, observations that come from looking at myself, my wife, my children; observations that come from letters, phone calls and emails to us at Good News Broadcasting; observations that I call the "facts of life" - how life works in the real world.

Observation Number 1: There is always some level of disappointment, even in the best of circumstances. Think about the best situations in your life and see if it isn't true. You're happy about what has happened. But you think, 'Maybe more could have happened. It could have been better." My point is that even on the best days, there is always something lacking.

Observation Number 2: Circumstances are rarely at their best. You know that's true. Your boss is never satisfied. Your friends forget to call you like they promised. There's a traffic jam on the way home from work. You struggle to get on the same wavelength as your spouse. Everywhere we look, there's a significant gap between what ought to be and what is, and day by day and hour by hour, that gap is cause for significant disappointment. But it gets even worse.

Observation Number 3: Life is often blatantly unfair. It's not a case of things just "not being at their best." We're talking about the deck being stacked against us for no apparent reason. It's not fair that some of us had to grow up with abusive parents while others did not. It's not fair that some of us have to battle physical and emotional illness while others just sail along. A lot of times, life is blatantly unfair.

Some of us choose to *deny the pain*. Just pretend that everything is okay. Don't think about that gap between what ought to be and what is in our marriage. Like the song said: "Don't worry, be happy." People who choose this path eventually become as shallow as that song was. They never go deeper than surface level issues, because to go under the surface is just too scary.

Perhaps as you read this you're saying. "Wait a minute, Derek - doesn't the Bible say we should be content in every circumstance?" Actually, Paul says, "I know what it is to be in need, and I know what it is to have plenty. I have learned the secret of being content in any and every situation." Paul didn't look at an empty cupboard and say, "I have plenty." Paul never denied it when he was disappointed. He said, "I've been in need. Things have been less than perfect." I am concerned that some of you are heading for disaster because you keep pretending that everything is okay, when it's not. Keep it up and you'll become little more than a plastic person who says all the right things on the outside and falls apart on the inside. You need a better strategy.

Other people *try to ease the pain*. They're aware of that gap between what is and what ought to be. They see it in the world. They experience it personally. And it hurts. So they try to drown it in pleasurable activities. They think "life is so hard. I deserve a little relief."

Here's how it works. Feel a little pain? Had a rough day at work? Wife been neglecting you? Reach for something sweet. Reach for a six-pack. Reach for something pornographic. Do whatever it takes to escape the reality of the misery of life, just for a little while. It's not hard to tell where that leads, is it? Since disappointment is a daily occurrence, this strategy risks addiction of one kind or another. You need a better strategy.

Some people **blame the pain on someone else**. They see the gap between what ought to be and what is and they say to themselves: "somebody is going to pay. In fact, everybody I come in contact with is going to pay." And they become bitter. Bitter towards the people around them and even bitter towards God. That's where some of you are today and it's the most dangerous place to be of all. You need a better strategy. And there is a better strategy.

God's strategy for disappointment says, 'Embrace the pain'. Stop denying it, stop pretending that "everything is just fine." Stop trying to ease it through some addictive behaviour. Stop blaming others. Instead, face it head on. Touch it. Feel it. Embrace it. Let it break your heart and let it drive you to the source of comfort. You will never know the depths of God's love for you, until you identify and fully embrace your disappointment with life.

In the years that I've been a pastor of a church I've seen more of the ugliness of life than I ever imagined existed. More and more, I'm coming to realise that I'm not personally going to change the world. People are going to come to a church, read a booklet like this and say, "Oh, it's so wonderful" - and continue right on down the path of destruction ... and there's not a thing I can do about it. Most people who contact me in a crisis will flatly ignore my advice. And those who do follow it - well, sometimes it doesn't work.

24

How we handle disappointments in life in many instances depends upon our understanding of God and it often boils down to the fact that we are disappointed with him. When you stop and consider why we're disappointed with God, it comes down to two questions that are difficult to answer.

The 'Why' and 'Where' questions of disappointment.

The most frequent question is the *"why?"* question: "Why did this happen?" *"*Why does an innocent child have to die at the hands of an abuser?" "Why does ...?" I'm sure that you have your own versions of the "why?" question.

According to Dr. James Dobson, in his book *When God Doesn't Make Sense,* it's the confusion over "why?" that shreds our faith. He writes: "The human spirit is capable of withstanding enormous discomfort, including the prospect of death, if the circumstances make sense. Many martyrs, political prisoners, and war heroes have gone to their graves willingly and confidently. They understood the sacrifice they were making and accepted its meaning in their lives .... Their attitude appears to be, 'the cause for which I'm risking my life is more than justified'." But, he concludes, those who become "confused and disillusioned with God have no such consolation. It is the absence of meaning that makes their situation so intolerable."

But there's another question, maybe even more troubling than the *"why?"* question. It's the *"where?"* question. "Where is God" while all this terrible stuff is happening? Why doesn't He do something? The greatest frustration is knowing that God could rescue, heal and could save. But why won't He do it? This sense of abandonment is a terrible experience especially for someone whose entire being is rooted in the Christian ethic. Satan then whispers, "He is not there! You are alone!" Ever felt like that?

Disappointment with God is rooted in the "why?" and "where?" questions that seemingly have no answer. So what are we to do when we come face to face with them? I think part of the answer is to focus on what we do know about God as opposed to what we don't know or understand. Here are four critical truths that we need to hang on to.

First of all, **God loves you**. We read in Romans 8:35, "Who shall separate us from the love of Christ?" At this point, I want to make it crystal clear to those of you who have been discouraged and defeated, overwhelmed by questions of "why?" and "where?" ... that God's heart is especially tender towards you. He knows your name. He has seen every tear you have cried. Every time life took a wrong turn, He was there.

Paul goes on to say "that neither death nor life, angels, demons, the present, the future, any powers, height, depth, nor anything else in all creation, will be able to separate us from the love of God that is in Christ Jesus our Lord." Anytime we are tempted to doubt God's love for us, we should always go back to the cross. If God loved me enough to give His Son to die for me when I was His enemy, surely He cannot fail to love me in my times of adversity. God loves you. Believe it.

But here's another fact to hold onto, **God is in control**, despite all appearances to the contrary. Theologians call this "the sovereignty of God." There's an interesting verse in Ecclesiastes 7, "When times are good, be happy; but when times are bad, consider: God has made the one as well as the other." So, does that mean that God actually caused something terrible to happen to you or me? This much can be said: Nothing happens to you or me unless God allows it. God isn't looking the other way or caught by surprise when adversity strikes. It may come from the hand of Satan, but God ultimately allows it. That's exactly what happened to Job. Everything that hit him was Satan's idea and Satan's doing. But he could do nothing to Job without God's permission.

But that raises yet another question: "Why would God allow terrible people and events into our lives?" One answer is that you and I choose to sin and sin brings death and destruction to the whole world. Since we choose to sin, God allows the consequences of that choice to play itself out. That's what the Bible says. But the Bible also teaches that God is a God of grace. He doesn't just leave us to suffer consequences. In His mercy towards those who follow Him, He actually turns senseless occurrences into events that have an ultimate purpose.

Here is that purpose, **God desires to deepen your faith**. According to the Bible, faith, "is being sure of what we hope for and certain of what we do not see." If you have all the answers - you don't need faith. In fact, the more answers you have, the less faith you need, and that's not good because, as that scripture goes on to say, "without faith it is impossible to please God."

The determination to believe when proof is not provided and questions are not answered is central to our relationship with God. God wants to deepen our faith and sometimes he uses pain to bring that about. God does not delight in bringing us pain and heartache. He always has a purpose for the grief He allows into our lives. Most often, we do not know what that purpose is, but it is enough to know that His infinite wisdom and perfect love have determined that the particular sorrow is best for us. God never wastes pain. He always uses it to accomplish his purpose.

There's a very old story which is worth telling again. Someone watched a moth struggle to free itself from its cocoon. In an effort to help - and not realising the necessity of the struggle - the viewer snipped the shell of the cocoon. Soon the moth came out with its wings all crimped and shrivelled. But as the person watched, the wings remained weak. What they didn't realise was that the struggle to emerge from the cocoon was an essential part of developing the muscle system of the moth's body. By seeking to cut short the moth's struggle, the person had actually crippled the moth and doomed its existence. The adversities of life are much like that cocoon. God uses them to develop the spiritual muscle system of our lives.

So, God loves you; God is in control; and God wants to deepen the faith of his followers. Those are moderately difficult truths to hold onto when you're in the midst of adversity. But the most difficult one is this: **God does not owe us answers**. "Why did this happen?" we ask. "Where was God?" we complain. As harsh as it may sound, it's God's prerogative to ignore those questions. We must never forget that He, after all, is God. He is accountable to no one. He is not a genie who pops out of the bottle to satisfy our whims. He is not our servant - we are His. Sometimes He performs mighty miracles on our behalf. Sometimes He chooses to explain His action in our lives. But at other times when nothing makes sense - when what we are going through is 'not fair' - He simply says, "I am God. Trust Me!"

But, you know, even if God did give us answers, I'm not sure it would make any difference because God says "As the heavens are higher than the earth, so are my ways higher than your ways and my thoughts than your thoughts."

Dobson tells the story of Jim Conway, a pastor whose young daughter developed a cancerous tumour on her leg. He and his wife prayed and prayed but, in the end, the leg had to be amputated. One of the church members came to Conway and said: "Pastor, I think God has allowed this to happen, because it has brought about a revival in our church." Conway said, "So, what is God going to do when this revival passes? Chop off Becki's other leg? Then her arm and her other arm?" His conclusion was, "when you start reaching for puny answers like that, it dehumanises those who suffer and insults God. I couldn't explain why Becki had to lose her leg, but I knew the answers being given weren't right."

We just don't have the mental and spiritual capacity to comprehend the meaning of all the circumstances of our lives. There is comfort in that because we are relieved from the responsibility of trying to figure them out.

It is not wrong to ask God the "why?" question. He may answer it, and good for you if He does. But at some point, we've got to stop asking "why?" and start asking "who?"

Who was in control? And when you start asking the "who?" question you do get answers - some incredibly stunning answers, like the God who loves us and is in control agrees to deals with Satan - for our benefit. That is beyond our understanding. Answers like the God who loves us and is in control puts up with the foolish rage of people like Job. That's beyond our comprehension. The God who loves us and is in control takes it upon Himself to bear the sin and sorrow of the world by getting nailed to a Roman cross. That is so far above us that words cannot express the mystery of God, other than to say as Job did. "My ears had heard of you, but now my eyes have seen you. Therefore I despise myself and repent in dust and ashes." Job was silenced by the magnitude of his foolishness. He conceded, "Surely, I spoke of things I did not understand, things too wonderful for me to know." That's what it feels like when the "Who?" question is answered.

Some of you are going through trials and tribulations today, and some of you will be going through them much sooner than you want to... and you're in trouble because you've confused the "who?" with the circumstances of life. If you and I confuse God with the physical reality of life - by expecting constant good health for example - then we set ourselves up for a crashing disappointment because life is not fair, and God is not life. Stop asking "why?" and start asking "who?" And then decide to obey God in spite of circumstances.

There's an interesting verse in the book of Deuteronomy that says, "There are secrets the Lord your God has not revealed to us, but these words that *He has revealed* are for us and our children to obey forever."

We don't know what God's sovereign will is. We do not know how He will arrange the circumstances of our future, whether favourably or unfavourably from our viewpoint. That's in the arena of the "secrets" that are not revealed to us. We do know that He will work to accomplish His purpose, which is ultimately for our good. Our duty then, is to obey the "words that he has revealed". To some of you who are struggling today, let me encourage you to change your focus from that which God will not reveal until Heaven... to what God has already revealed... and obey it.

The bottom line in handling disappointment.

I can tell you that the best way to handle disappointment with God is to admit that your ability to understand is limited; to stop focusing on the "why?" and start focusing on the "who?"; and to obey what God has already revealed to you. But you'll never do those things until you get one issue straight.

Look at the end of verse 5 in Romans 8: "Those who live in accordance with the Spirit have their minds set on what the Spirit desires." In other words, "make acknowledging the Lord in our thinking the focus of all that we are and do."

Jim Conway, in dealing with the tragedy that had struck his daughter, came to this conclusion: "I became deeply aware that there were only two choices that I could make. One was to continue in my anger at God and follow the path of despair I was on. The other choice was to let God be God and somehow say, 'I don't know how all of this fits together. I don't understand the reasons for it. I'm not even going to ask for the explanation. I've chosen to accept the fact that you are God and I'm the servant, not the other way around'."

"It was in that choice," he writes, "that I came to cope with my situation. I frankly admit that after all these years, I still struggle with some things. But I have come to recognise that God has a higher purpose and I just don't understand that purpose. I am prepared to wait until eternity to receive answers to my questions, if necessary. Like Job, I am now able to say, "though he slay me, yet will I trust in him." It's either despair, or it's the acceptance of [God's] sovereignty. Those are the alternatives... there is nothing in between."

And that's the bottom line on this issue: It's a choice of trust or despair. Are we going to trust the God who loves us, who's in control, who wants to deepen our faith - or are we going to live a life of despair over questions that we can't answer? I hope for your own sake you'll choose to trust.

The promise of a stress free life and a God who always does what He is told is a myth! Instead we find One who says, "Let me be God. Trust in Me with all your heart and don't depend on your ability to figure everything out." But as disappointed as I might be with life in general and with a God who wants to do it His way instead of my way, the truth is... I'm just as disappointed with me. I'm not the kind of person I should be. I'm not the person I want to be.

The gap between what is and what ought to be in this world seems even larger when I honestly look at myself. I contribute to it - every day. I add to my own disappointment with life. But what's really disappointing is that there are times when it seems that I'm doomed to always be less than I want to be or ought to be. I say that because a frank appraisal of my life reveals two characteristics that I can't deny or explain away.

Firstly, the pattern of my life reveals that **I am captive to sin**. My life is summed up in a few sentences that are found in Paul's letter to the church at Rome: "I really want to do what is right, but I can't." Says Paul, "In my mind I want to be God's willing servant, but instead I find myself still enslaved to sin." How about you? Have you ever noticed this tendency in yourself? I think if you were honest, you'd have to say "Yes Derek, there's a part of me that's captive to sin, too."

Secondly, I've noticed that **positive change comes very slowly in this life**. Sometimes I look at myself and I ask: "How can it be, after all this time, that the gap between what is and what ought to be in my life is still so wide? Why does it take so long for me to get where I want to be in my relationship with God, with my family, in my personal character ... but only an instant to "fall off the wagon"? Real change - positive change - seems to take forever. And the truth is, that some things about me won't change until I die and "forever" begins. I don't know about you, but when I put that observation together with the fact that part of me is captive to sin, it can be pretty demoralising. I begin to have thoughts like: "Why bother? I mean, I'm never going to close that gap between what is and what ought to be in myself. Sin drags me down. Change is slow. Why even try? Why not just give in and go with the flow?" Those thoughts reveal the magnitude of the problem: If I don't deal with it in the right way, disappointment with myself can discourage me to the point of quitting. And it can discourage you, too. In fact, some of you are so disappointed in yourself, so discouraged, thinking, "What's the use? The gap between what is and what ought to be in me is so huge I'll never be able to close it." You're ready to quit. But you and I don't have to. We can learn to deal with the disappointment in ourselves in a way that encourages us instead of discourages us.

As Paul writes to the believers in Rome who could be tempted to give up and go with the flow. In no uncertain terms, he challenges them and through them, us: Don't do it! Don't give up! Don't quit! And he gave them this insight in Romans 8: "If we are the children of God, then we are heirs – heirs of God and co-heirs with Christ. . . I consider that our present sufferings are not worth comparing with the glory that will be revealed in us."

Notice not 'to us' but 'in us'! We have a future. You can put up with today's disappointments when you put it into the perspective of eternal glory. That's why Paul goes on to say, "keep your hope in God. 'All things' ,even the bad things, 'will work for the good'," it doesn't say that they *are good* but "*work for the good*, of those who love Him, who have been called according to his purpose." Don't let the fact that you know that verse well deprive you of its help. Let's keep our hope in God. How do you do that? Where do you find the stamina to keep going? I think there are five things that we can do to keep our disappointment from discouraging us to the point of quitting.

Preventing disappointment turning into discouragement.

First of all, and this is prerequisite to everything else I'll say: **Accept God's grace**, his undeserved favour towards us, in Jesus. Remember how the Apostle Paul described the frustration with his "sin gap"? He said, "In my mind I want to be God's willing servant, but instead I find myself still enslaved to sin."

Read his conclusion on the matter: "Who will free me from my slavery to this deadly lower nature? Thank God! It has been done by Jesus Christ our Lord. He has set me free. So there is NOW NO CONDEMNATION AWAITING THOSE WHO BELONG TO CHRIST JESUS. For the power of the life-giving Spirit - and this power is mine through Christ Jesus - has freed me from the vicious circle of sin and death."

Do you see what he's saying? Freedom from the tyranny of the "sin gap" comes through Jesus. As long as we wallow in our failures, we allow them to "hinder us and entangle us" and we become discouraged and defeated. But when you and I can look at that gap in our lives and say, "yes, it is there but there is no condemnation for it, because I belong to Jesus and God covered my sin gap in his grace when Jesus died on the cross." When you can say those things, it makes a huge difference on how you deal with the disappointment in yourself. It doesn't go away, but you don't get discouraged to the point of giving up.

Now, I'm not saying, "ignore the gap; don't let it bother you." That's just playing a game of pretend. We don't need to deny our shortcomings. Instead, we need to come to Jesus and admit, "I've disobeyed the laws of a holy and righteous God and I deserve condemnation but You, Jesus, paid the penalty for me through Your death on the cross, and I accept that for me, personally." That's what it means to accept God's grace in Jesus. There are some of us who have already done that, but we've forgotten what it means. We've forgotten that God's grace to us in Jesus means that there's no condemnation for the gap in our lives. To you I say, stop wallowing in your disappointment and start rejoicing that you've been set free.

Secondly, to avoid becoming so discouraged that you want to quit, you've got to **believe in God's vision for you**. If you are a follower of Christ, do you know what God's vision is for your life? The Apostle Paul describes it this way: "We know that the whole creation has been groaning as in the pains of childbirth right up to the present time. Not only so, but we ourselves groan inwardly as we wait eagerly for our adoption as children, the redemption of our bodies."

Paul is saying that something incredible is waiting to be birthed in you and me. And it's not an easy labour. It's a slow painful process. But here it is, "For those God foreknew he also predestined to be *conformed to the likeness of His Son."* In other words, God's vision for you is that you become like Jesus! God loves you the way you are - that's His grace - but He loves you too much to leave you that way - that's His vision.

One day the gap between what is and what ought to be in the lives of Christ's followers will be closed. Permanently. If you follow Christ, Paul says that God will continually arrange all the circumstances of your life to "conform you" into the likeness of His character. And let me tell you, knowing that - believing in God's vision for your life - makes all the difference in the world. Because when you know where you're heading, disappointment with where you are today won't discourage you to the point of quitting.

So, accept God's grace in Jesus, believe in God's vision for you. Remember it's not a sprint, **the Christian life is a marathon**. As Paul says about our hope in Romans 8, we have to wait patiently for it. Often, people expect their faith in Christ to make them spiritually mature overnight. The fact is that becoming a follower of Christ doesn't mean an automatic change in your behaviour. Spiritual growth and the change associated with that growth come as a result of a process. And that process is a marathon, not a sprint. In a marathon, runners have some good stretches and some bad stretches. It's part of the deal. They don't quit over it. They just keep running. The same is true in the race of following Christ. There are times when you will see great spiritual growth in your life. And then there are other times when you look at the gap between what is and what ought to be in your life and you'll think, "what's the use?" And you'll quit unless you remember that it's not a sprint, it's a marathon.

Here's the attitude of a person who's running a spiritual marathon: "Let us not get tired of doing what is right, for after a while we will reap a harvest of blessing if we don't get discouraged and give up" (Galatians 6:9). Just keep running. It will make a difference. In the Christian life, how you finish is much more important than how you start.

That leads to the next idea: Don't try to be like Jesus, **train to be like Jesus**. Did you know that marathon runners don't try to run the race? They train to run it. Becoming like Jesus - seeing the 'what is' and 'what ought to be' gap in your life eventually narrow - works the same way. It doesn't happen just because you try hard to do what's right. It happens because you train hard. That's what the apostle Paul was talking about when he wrote to the Corinthians, "So run your race to win."

When you and I engage in spiritual training - when we make it a habit to do those things that help us grow, things like being in church, participating in a small group, reading the Bible and praying on our own, serving, and giving - we will see progress, When we make it a habit to avoid that which leads us into sin - certain situations or people - when we train in that way, we will see progress. Seeing progress helps us to avoid the discouragement that tempts us to give up. Now, having said that, I need to also say that no matter how much training we do, we are not going to reach perfection on this earth. The gap may narrow, but it will always be with us.

Hang on for heaven! This last piece of advice is so important: Again as Paul says to the Romans, God has you in a chain of command. He has put His hand upon you to make you His own. He has justified you and those He accepts and gives the status of being in the right with Him through Christ, "He also glorifies." So, hang in there, don't be discouraged, don't quit. Heaven is coming for those who follow Christ.

How do you handle that disappointment with yourself? Do you just blow it off - "Oh, my life's okay. I mess up now and then, but I just go on." If so, you are just playing a game, a very dangerous one. Or, are you resigned to give up and go with the flow because, "I'm a captive to sin and positive change comes so slowly"?

If that's where you are, let me encourage you - don't quit! Don't throw in the towel. Accept the grace of God in Jesus that covers your sins and failures. Stop believing that you're doomed and start believing in the vision that God has for you, the vision that says that one day you will have the character of Jesus formed within you.

Remind yourself that life is a marathon and it's okay that change doesn't happen overnight. Start training to be like Jesus and, finally, set your sights on heaven. Set your sights on that day when God's work in you will be completed and the gap between what is and what ought to be is no more.

Chapter 3
Conquering Boredom

A ten-year-old boy was asked, "What do you want to be when you grow up?" Influenced by terrorist attacks, the boy thought for a moment and then replied with just one word: "Alive."

I guess that all of us join him in his wish.

The love of life lies deep in us. Jesus summed up His mission to earth with these famous words: "I am come that they might have life, and that they might have it more abundantly." One man said that he used to hate getting up in the morning because he didn't like his own life. Negativity had gripped him so deeply that he didn't care if he lived or died. Then he met Jesus. "Now I love my life. I love my family and I love my work. I'm overwhelmed everyday. I know that Christians are supposed to look forward to heaven, but I don't want to die yet because I'm having so much fun." Yet many people, including many Christians, are utterly bored with life. One survey reports that 54% of us go to work primarily to escape the boredom of life at home. 70% of teenagers say they are bored with school. The survey also reported that 25% of teenagers say they got drunk at the weekend because they were so bored; they need a 'buzz'. Boredom is a combination of weariness, listlessness, apathy and unconcern that causes a person to feel like doing nothing. Related words include dreariness, flatness, lethargy, and dullness. To the bored person, the world is all shades of grey. When you are bored, there is nothing to do because there is nothing to do that matters. To the younger generation, one word has encapsulated boredom, the all-purpose answer was, "Whatever." "Did you hear what I said?" "Whatever." "I thought that was a great movie." "Whatever." The word "whatever" in that sense means, "I don't even care enough to give you an answer."

The primary causes of boredom.

Over stimulation.

We live in a society that encourages us to believe that more is better. If a little of anything is good, then more will always be better. If one drink is good, two is better, and five will send you to heaven. If one pill helps, two is a kicker, three is a party, and five will knock you out. We see this in relationships as people jump from one person to another. We see it in the pressure to constantly move "up the ladder", so people hop from one job to another, hoping to find the perfect fit. We move from city to city and from church to church. We make friends, keep them for a while, get to know them, and then we move on to someone else.

Advertisers prey on this tendency when they urge us to buy more, buy new, and buy now. We are so bombarded with images, with lights and sound and noise that we've grown accustomed to it. We are so over-stimulated by TV, radio, music, movies, the internet, and by video games, that we are hyped up, tense, wound up tight, and as a result, easily bored and quickly distracted.

Under commitment.

This is partly a result of the massive over stimulation. Too many people live at the 20% level of commitment. We are like the man who, when asked what he believed, replied, "A little bit of everything." We are like customers in a cafeteria line. We have a "little of this" and a "little of that" and not much of anything. We are 20% committed to our marriage, 20% committed to our work, 20% committed to our relationships, 20% committed to our families, 20% committed to our careers, 20% committed to our church, and we end up being 20% committed to Jesus Christ. No wonder we are frustrated. No wonder we are bored. We aren't committed enough to anything to find a reason to get out of bed in the morning. Underneath all this is a deeper problem.

Excessive self-focus.

Bored people are essentially selfish people who view the universe through their own stunted perspective. The reason we are bored is because we have become boring people. To be truthful, we are bored with ourselves. The problem is not "out there" somewhere. Look inside if you want the answer. Lest I be misunderstood, I do not think 'busyness' is the answer to boredom. Busy people are often very bored. They use their 'busyness' to mask their inner emptiness.

I was teaching at a Bible School and the question came up, "Is boredom a sin?" Good question. After contemplating the matter, I think the answer is that sin and boredom go together, but I would rather say that boredom is a disease. It is a warning sign from God that there is a *"dis-ease"* in your heart that must be faced. Boredom is a sign that your life is moving in the wrong direction.

Overcoming boredom.

It requires a reorientation of the way we approach each day. You would never think of the apostle Paul as a bored man. But do you realise that he spent many weeks languishing in dungeons? He knew what it was to not have his plans work out, to go into a 'holding pattern' in life. For a 'go-getter' like Paul that would have been tough. And yet he could write to the church in Rome which he longed to visit, and had been prevented again and again from doing so, that he wanted to 'refresh' these believers and be 'refreshed' by them in return. There was nothing dry and stale about Paul. There was nothing that made you say, "Oh no, spending time with him, that will be as interesting as watching paint dry!"

A key verse is Romans 8:37 where Paul looks back over tough times, tired times, tedious times and tense times; and what does he say? "In all these things we are more than conquerors through him who loved us." Literally we can become *super conquerors,* or what we're calling in this booklet, an 'over-conqueror'. Why? Because whatever happens in our lives can make us draw closer to Christ. It makes us cling harder. Christ has all the love, joy, peace, and so much more that makes life work well.

In order to find a Biblical answer to boredom, I'd like to combine two verses – Ecclesiastes 9:10 which says, 'Whatever your hand finds to do, do it with all your might, for in the grave, where you are going, there is neither working nor planning nor knowledge nor wisdom' and Colossians 3:17, ' And whatever you do, whether in word or deed, do it all in the name of the Lord Jesus, giving thanks to God the Father through him.'

We overcome boredom by doing whatever lies close at hand.

"Whatever your hand finds to do" says the writer of Ecclesiastes. Eugene Peterson's translation, The Message, offers a punchier version of this phrase: "Whatever turns up, grab it and do it." I like that because it emphasises the unpredictable nature of life. No matter how well planned your day may be, something unexpected is always bound to "turn up". When it does, grab it and do it. That's good advice. The deeper meaning of this phrase challenges us to take hold of the ordinary responsibilities of life and make sure they get done. It's easy for any of us to live in the never-never land of what we plan to do tomorrow. We dream about starting a diet or getting a new job, buying a new computer or meeting the person of our dreams. Or, somehow finishing that term paper, or painting the living room, or learning Spanish, or calling on a new client. Or, applying for a grant or going back to college, or any of a thousand other worthwhile ideas. Meanwhile, there is work to be done, much of it tedious, that somehow gets left undone while we are dreaming about what we are going to do "someday." Unfortunately, someday never comes for many people.

"One good deed is worth more than a thousand brilliant theories", said Charles Haddon Spurgeon. Better to do what you need to do than to waste four hours dreaming about what you would like to do. When Solomon says, "Whatever your hand finds to do", he doesn't mean, "If your hand happens to find something to do, do it, and if not, then take the day off and watch TV." No! Your hand will always find something to do. There is always work to be done. That's what life is - a whole bunch of duties large and small that "someone" has to do. It won't do to complain and say, "I don't feel like doing it." Your feelings don't matter. Whatever your hand finds to do, do it! This is the Word of God. We all have work to do; we all have chores, jobs, responsibilities, assignments in life. No one gets a free ride. You can't stay in bed forever.

There is a further implication here. One of the best cures for boredom is to get involved helping others. One doctor said that whenever a patient complains of vague symptoms with no medical cause, he tells them to "crawl out of yourself." It means to crawl out of the cave of self-pity and get involved in the world of hurting people.

Recently I watched a TV special on the life of Prince Charles. The documentary noted that Charles was devastated by the death of his great-uncle, Lord Mountbatten, who was murdered by the Irish Republican Army in 1979. Lord Mountbatten was the only man who had truly been a father figure to Charles. After the death of his mentor, Charles consoled himself by recalling the advice his great-uncle had given him. "Banish your sorrow through service to others", he told young Charles. That is very wise counsel.

Famed psychiatrist Karl Menninger was once asked, "What should you do if you feel a nervous breakdown coming on?" Everyone expected him to say, "See a psychiatrist", but he replied, "Lock the door of your house, go across the railroad tracks, find someone in need and do something to help that person."

You've probably seen the following quotation many times. It's over 200 years old and comes originally from the Quakers.
"I expect to pass through the world but once.
Any good therefore that I can do,
or any kindness that I can show to any fellow creature,

let me do it now.
Let me not defer or neglect it,
for I shall not pass this way again."

It is very difficult to be bored when you are giving yourself to help those around you. Boredom comes when we focus on our own needs. Crawl outside yourself and your problems will seem smaller and your boredom will soon disappear.

We overcome boredom by doing our work with passion.

"Do it with all your might" says Ecclesiastes. Not only are we to do whatever lies close at hand, we are to tackle our work with gusto. The Puritans talked often about the importance of earnestness. That's an old word, one we don't hear much nowadays, but it perfectly describes how Christians should approach life. Life is too short, too fragile, and too precious to take lightly. Whatever we do, we should do it heartily, with enthusiasm, with passion, with zeal, with 100% commitment.

Most of us don't approach our work that way. If you want to see how many people view their work, watch an episode of "The Simpsons." To Homer Simpson, work is a joke, a place to goof off, a place where nothing really matters, and where breaking the rules is the order of the day. It's very telling that whenever Marge wants to have a serious talk with Homer about shaping up, he responds by saying, "Boring". How different that is from the biblical view of work, which is that all work is noble if it is done for the glory of God. Even the most mundane task is worthwhile if we do it in the right spirit. Martin Luther said that a dairymaid can milk cows to the glory of God. If your job is shovelling manure, then do your best and shovel that manure for the glory of God, and if you do it well, you honour God just as much as the brain surgeon who saves someone's life.

We all struggle with this on one level or another. Society tells us that some jobs matter more than others. Certainly some jobs pay more than others and some jobs gain much more praise than others. It's easy to fall into the trap of saying, "I hate my job. I don't feel good. I don't like the place where I work. I'm surrounded by idiots. My boss hates me. The woman next to me is so catty. The pay is lousy. No one likes me. And besides, I've got a bad cough and a headache." Poor baby. I'm sure that everything you've just said is true. Why should I doubt you? The biblical answer is: Grow up!

You're not supposed to like your job every day. It's not supposed to be fun all the time. That's why they call it work. If work was supposed to be fun all the time, it would be spelled F-U-N. Many days you won't feel like going to work, and if you go, you won't enjoy it. Big deal. Go anyway. Do what you have to do. And do it with all your heart. Put your passion into your job and see what happens. Read the text again. It doesn't say, "Do it with all your might if you feel like it." Or "Do it with all your might if you enjoy it." Or "Do it with all your might if they treat you right." God says, "Do it with all your might even when you don't feel like it, you don't like it, and you don't want to be there. And then leave everything else in my hands."

There is a huge theological truth underlying this principle. If you believe in the sovereignty of God, then it must be true that you are where you are because God wants you to be there, because if God didn't want you to be there, you would be somewhere else. But since you are where you are right now, that must be because you are there by God's design and when he wants you to be somewhere else, that's where you'll be. If you believe that, then you can do your work each day, even in a very bad situation, as unto the Lord, with all your might, for his glory.

We overcome boredom by pondering the brevity of life.

Ecclesiastes puts it like this: "For in the grave, where you are going, there is neither working nor planning nor knowledge nor wisdom." Although the first half of this verse is justly famous and often quoted, the last half is virtually unknown. It's easy to see why that is so since it appears to be such a downer. Who wants to hear that they are going to the grave? That's a fact we'd all rather ignore. There is a different translation of this verse in the Contemporary

English Version: "Work hard at whatever you do. You will soon go to the world of the dead, where no one works or thinks or reasons or knows anything." That makes the hair stand up on your neck doesn't it? "You will soon go to the world of the dead" sounds like something you would find in a bad Chinese fortune cookie. But it is entirely true whether we like it or not. We're all going to the land of the dead sooner or later.

As I thought about this, my mind drifted back to a little incident that happened a few years ago. My wife, Pauline went with a young widow to make arrangements for the burial of her husband. The Funeral Director said, "We'll arrange for a double plot!" The young widow asked "Why double?" He looked a little embarrassed and mumbled it was a place for her! Pauline said she thought the man had been doing his job too long because he wasn't at all sensitive to the feelings of the widow, but of course, the man was right. There is always room for someone else in the cemetery.

The old joke goes like this: Why is there a fence around the cemetery? Answer: Because people are dying to get in. I understand the comment of the man who said this: "Everyone should go to one wedding and one funeral each year. The wedding gives you hope for the future and the funeral reminds you that so much of what we worry about doesn't really matter." Life is not a dress rehearsal. We only get one chance to do whatever we're going to do on planet earth. Soon enough, sooner than we think, our moment in the sun will be over.

Do you recall how on September 11, 2001, after the planes hit the Pentagon and the World Trade Center, millions of people picked up the phone to call each other? Parents called children, brothers called sisters, friends called friends, long-lost relatives called to make sure everyone was okay. One of the ironies of it all is that it takes a tragedy to force us to face the brevity of life.

Do not think you are immortal. When you die, we'll take your body, put it in a box, and we'll put the box in the ground.

We're all going to do some serious "box time" before it's over. No one will escape "the box" unless you happen to live until the rapture. The point is, do whatever you're going to do now. If you intend to do some good deed, do it now. If you have some great plan, work on it now. If you intend to do something or be something or try something, do it or be it or try it now. You don't have time to be bored. You can take it easy in "the box." What I am saying is precisely the meaning of Ecclesiastes 9:10. Martin Luther said a man should live with the day of his death on a placard before his eyes. Luther managed to turn the world upside down. I wish that we had the same realistic view of life and death.

We overcome boredom by remembering we represent Jesus in everything we do.

Paul's words to the Colossians make that clear. "Whatever you do, whether in word or deed, do it all in the name of the Lord Jesus." The New Living Translation puts it this way: "And whatever you do or say, let it be as a representative of the Lord Jesus." What if you had to sign your name to everything you said and everything you did? Suppose that somehow a nametag attached to every one of your actions - good and bad - so that everyone could see who did it: Tom, Dick or Harry! Sometimes we are sloppy about what we say and do precisely because we don't think anyone notices what we are doing.

Let's take this a step further. What if Jesus had to sign His name to everything you say and everything you do? For every careless word, the name "Jesus Christ" was attached. And for every careless complaint, the name "Jesus Christ" was attached. That might stop us in our tracks if we thought His name was attached to our words and our deeds. Here's the kicker: His name is attached to our words and deeds because His name is attached to us! We are "Jesus people" who claim to walk the "Jesus road." We call Him our Master, our Saviour and our Lord. We tell the world that we have left everything to take up our cross and follow Him. We even call ourselves "Christians" - "Christ-followers."

Whether we like it or not, His name attaches to everything we say, even the foolish remarks, the unkind words, the angry insults, the swear words, the threats we utter, and all the rest. His name attaches to our complaints, our excuses, our boasts, our lies, our flattery, our moral compromise, our laziness, our dishonesty, and even to the worst sins that we can commit. If we go into a brothel, the name of Jesus goes with us. If we steal money, the name of Jesus goes with us. If we abuse our children, the name of Jesus gets dragged down with us. We would be more concerned about the details of life if we remembered that we are the face of Jesus on the earth today. We like to say that Jesus is the light of the world, and He is. But we are also the light of the world. As the saying goes, we're the only Bible some people will ever read, and we're the only Jesus some people will ever see.

We overcome boredom by being thankful for things large and small.

There is one final way to avoid boredom - by cultivating a thankful heart in all the circumstances of life. Colossians 3:17 says, "Giving thanks to God the Father through Him." It's amazing how well this correlates with the context of Ecclesiastes 9. If you go back and read verses 6 to 9, you discover that the writer urges us to enjoy the simple pleasures of life. You're going to die soon so... enjoy your food and drink, dress up and smell good, enjoy your wife and the pleasures of married life. All these things are gifts from God. They are simple pleasures - food and drink, nice clothes, a happy marriage. This is not hedonism - far from it. This is taking pleasure in the daily blessings of God.

Here's a suggestion. Why not find a day to spend two hours doing nothing but giving thanks to God? To most of us, the idea sounds foreign because we're so over-stimulated already that we can't slow down enough to spend that much time giving thanks. Many of us would rattle off a few things and be done with our thanksgiving in five minutes. Then it's on to the next thing on the agenda.

Here's how you do it. Think about your eyes. Give thanks for the parts of your eyes that God's providence keeps in good working order. Thank Him for the birds that fly overhead, the clouds that float in the sky, the snow that falls in the winter, the brilliant colours of the sunset, and the rain that waters the soil. If you think about it, you could spend two hours right there. Then go to your ears, your nose, your sense of smell, your sense of taste, the things you touch with your hands, and the places you go with your feet. Think about your friends and family and give thanks for them by name, one by one. Stop from time to time to sing praises to the Lord. The two hours will fly by. And when it is over, your heart will be refreshed and you will come away realising how much you already have.

Folk singer Joan Baez once remarked, "You don't get to choose how you're going to die, or when. You can only decide how you're going to live now." If you are bored, it is because you have chosen to live a boring life. Boredom is not an issue of bad circumstances. It's a disease of the soul caused by excessive self-focus. And it comes from being over-stimulated and under-committed. Life is never boring when you commit wholly to Jesus Christ.

Are you bored with life?

Crawl out of yourself and make a new commitment to the Lord. Reach outside yourself to help someone less fortunate and your perspective on life will radically change. Boredom is a warning sign that we are living for self when we ought to be living for God.

For many of us, the issue is this: Have you ever committed yourself 100% to Jesus? As long as we live at the 20% level, we will be miserable, unhappy, frustrated, angry, upset and bored. There is no one unhappier than a 20% Christian. I want to call out all the 20% husbands. The 20% fathers, the 20% wives. The 20% children, and all the folks who give 20% at work, 20% to their careers, 20% at school, 20% in the youth group, 20% at church, 20% to your ministry, and 20% to Jesus Christ. It's time to give 100% in every area of life. God bless every Christian who joins the "100% Club." Commit all your ways to Jesus and your life will never be boring.

Boredom comes from living on our own strength within the confines of our own capacities. There needs to be some area or relationship in our lives in which we are attempting the humanly impossible. Robert Browning was right:
"A man's reach must exceed his grasp
Or what's a heaven for?"

What are you reaching for that exceeds your grasp? What are you attempting that can't be pulled off without a mighty intervention and invasion of the Holy Spirit's power? We all need (like the apostle Paul) a bit of danger, a careless daring, if we are to battle with boredom and win. What have we got to lose? Every courageous Christian who would escape the boredom of the traditional and the drab of the mundane needs a stretching commitment to do the impossible for Christ in some problem in society or with a problem person. We can easily discover what needs doing or saying if we will listen to our complaints about people, churches, or government. "What are we going to do about it?" silences a lot of fruitless and futile theorising. To confront, attack, and become involved (in Christ's name and by His Spirit's power) in the solution of a problem heals the boredom that no new job, spouse, or environment will ever cure.

Can I give you a personal word? I was bored until I turned my life over to the adventuresome management of Jesus Christ. Like Paul in Romans 8, I have become 'convinced' of something too. Living with the Saviour as Lord and leader has led me into mind-boggling, soul-stretching, spirit-enlightened challenges, and I have never been bored. He replaced my human ambitions with spiritual adventure. My passion has been, and ever will be, to care for people and introduce them to the Saviour. Edna St. Vincent Millay expressed my commitment to live all the years of my life:
"My candle burns at both ends;
It will not last the night;
But ah, my foes, and oh, my friends –
It gives a lovely light!"

There's so much to do, so much left unsaid, so much that's ambiguous or untrue that needs to be challenged. There are so many people who may expire without the opportunity to decide whether they want to live forever. How could life ever be boring with an impelling challenge like that?

Moss Hart gives us a motto for a thrilling life in his play, 'Light Up The Sky'. One of the characters called 'Sydney' talks about his excitement and expectation for a show about to open: "We're sticking a Roman candle into the tired face of show business tonight... and the sparks that fly are going to light up the theatre like an old-fashioned 4th of July." That's what we should be about - lighting the darkness, sticking a Roman candle into the tired face of boredom whenever and in whomever we find it. Boredom will be a thing of the past if we spend ourselves being sure no one around us is bored.

You may have resisted the idea that your life is boring. It may never have occurred to you that the blandness, dullness, and sameness of your life - the ruts of routine - are really boredom. But if life isn't exciting, if you don't feel a sense of adventure, if you're not delighted by the possibilities of tomorrow, if you've given up to the eventuality of sameness, then you're bored.

This could be the last day of boredom for you. Discover the joy of an intimate relationship with Christ. Become a celebrant of yourself, other people, and life. Lose yourself in people and their needs. Dare the impossible. Expect the surprising infusion of the Holy Spirit - and I can assure you that you'll never be bored again. Then you can rejoice with Christ, *the life,* and say with Paul, "In all things we are more than conquerors through Him who loved us."

Chapter 4
Conquering Discontentment

"I am disillusioned," a woman confided.

Her Pastor replied, "Wonderful!"

She said, "I don't think you heard me. I said that I am really disillusioned."

"Congratulations!" he said.

Well the woman was becoming perturbed. Then he explained. The real meaning of the word 'disillusioned' is to be set free of illusions. No one wants to live with illusions about life, people, or situations. An illusion is an impression, which misrepresents reality. It's a false impression or delusion. The Latin, *'illusio'*, means mocking or deceit. It's a blessing to be liberated from illusions. Disillusionment is a gift.

The word *'disillusion'* is one of our most misunderstood and misused words. We know what the woman meant. She had been disappointed to discover that she had been living with false expectations and dreams about people. She had been confronted with reality. How much better to live in the real world. That is what the apostle Paul was doing when he wrote to the Church in Rome. He faced the reality (as verse 36 in Romans 8 puts it quoting the Psalms) "For your sake we face death all day long; we are considered as sheep to be slaughtered." Is he disillusioned? Paul says emphatically, "No, in all these things we are more than conquerors through Him who loved us." Paul is convinced that nothing will separate him from Christ and His love. The word that he uses for 'more than conquerors' we're paraphrasing *'over-conqueror'*, in other words not letting life's circumstances get us down and destroy us.

Ever since the beginning of creation, when the first creatures came from the hand of God, there has always been someone, somewhere, unhappy with his position in the universe. It all started with an angel named Lucifer, the brightest star of the heavenly firmament, who was not satisfied to be the apex of God's creation. He wanted something more than his assigned position as the greatest of all created beings. His seething discontentment caused him to lead a rebellion against the Most High. Fully one-third of the angels joined with him in his abortive quest to overthrow the Throne of the Lord. For his rebellion, he and his followers were kicked out of heaven. Ever since that dark day, he has been known as Satan and the devil, and he has been the implacable foe of God and all his works.

It was discontentment that made him do it. And discontentment has been one of his best weapons ever since. His earliest triumph came in the Garden of Eden when he sowed seeds of discontentment in Eve's unsuspecting heart. By misquoting the Lord, he made Eve think that God was somehow trying to cheat her, to keep her down, to keep her from becoming "like God." So Eve took the fruit and ate it. She gave it to Adam and he ate it. Thus sin entered the human bloodstream. The seeds of discontentment brought forth the bitter harvest of disobedience, which led to the loss of paradise and the entrance of evil into our world. Ever since then we have been an unhappy race. After Eden we have never been fully satisfied with anything on earth. And we're still not satisfied thousands of years later. We always want something different. If we're young, we want to be older. If we're old, we wish we were younger. If it's old, we want something new. If it's new, we want something newer. If it's small, we want something bigger. If it's big, we want something really big. If we have a hundred pounds, we want two hundred. If we have two hundred, we want five hundred. If we have an apartment, we want a house. If we have a house, we want a bigger house, or a new house, or a nicer house. Or maybe we want to scale down and live in an apartment again. If we have a job, we dream of a better job, a bigger job, a closer job, with a bigger office, a better boss, better benefits, more challenge, bigger opportunity, nicer people to work for, and more vacation time. If we're single, we dream of being married. If we're married . . . you get the idea.

None of this is unusual in any way. We were born discontented and some of us stay that way forever. A certain amount of discontentment can be good for the soul. It's not wrong to have dreams about what the future might hold; the hope of something better drives us forward and keeps us working, inventing, striving, creating and innovating. But there is a kind of discontentment that leads in a wrong direction.

Here are five signs that discontentment is dragging us down spiritually:

1) *Envy.* The inability to rejoice at the success of others.
2) *Uncontrolled Ambition.* The desire to win at all costs, no matter what it takes or who gets trampled in the process.
3) *Critical Spirit.* The tendency to make negative, hurtful, cutting remarks about others.
4) *Complaining Spirit.* The disposition to make excuses and to blame others or bad circumstances for our problems. A refusal to take personal responsibility. Inability to be thankful for what we already have.
5) *Outbursts of Anger.* Angry words spoken because our expectations were not met.

The discontented person looks around and says, "I deserve something better than this." Because he is never happy and never satisfied, he drags others into the swamp with him. No wonder Benjamin Franklin declared, *"Contentment makes a poor man rich, discontent makes a rich man poor."* Discontentment is the cancer of the soul. It eats away our joy, corrodes our happiness, destroys our outlook on life, and produces a terminal jaundice of the soul so that everything looks negative to us. We cannot be happy because we will not be happy. We cannot be satisfied because we will not be satisfied. Such a person is truly a lost soul - miserable today and miserable tomorrow.

How can we overcome this debilitating condition?

The answer (as always) lies with good theology. Sin always stems from wrong thinking about God, about us, and about life in general. The one thing you can clearly say about the apostle Paul as he writes to the Church in Rome is this: There was plenty in his life to be discontented about. Not much had been working out as he expected or wanted. But, he could write it and mean it, "In all these things we are more than conquerors through Him who loved us." That's verse 37 in Romans 8, and it's our keynote verse for this book.

1 Corinthians 7 contains some amazingly helpful insights about discontentment even though the word itself is never used. This chapter is unique in that it was written by the Apostle Paul in answer to some specific questions put to him by the believers in the church at Corinth. One problem we have is that this chapter contains Paul's answers, but not the original questions. We have to infer the question by studying the context. We know in a general way that the Corinthians asked about marriage, divorce and singleness. The middle section of this chapter contains some excellent teaching on these topics that applies directly to the question of contentment versus discontentment. Consider four principles that will help us face and overcome the problem of discontentment.

One: You are where you are by God's assignment.

The first principle is repeated three times in this paragraph, verses 17 to 24: "Nevertheless, each one should retain the place in life that the Lord assigned to him and to which God has called him." "Each one should remain in the situation which he was in when God called him." "Brothers, each man, as responsible to God, should remain in the situation God called him to."

This is a case where the meaning is very clear: Lead the life God assigns to you. God has given each of us a job to do. He has gifted each person in a certain way and has assigned us a particular place in life. This reflects a very high view of God's sovereignty. We are both assigned and called to a certain place in life. The Greek words are very strong and definite. The old Puritans used to say, "God *orders* everything with perfect wisdom." I wonder how many of us would say that. Almost unconsciously, we want to change "everything" to "some things" or "a few things" or even "most things." But *"everything?"* Isn't that going too far? What about all the pain and suffering and evil in the world? How can that be "ordered" by God? Either we can talk about that for the next seventy years and still not settle it, or we can simply say that if God doesn't "order" all things, then He's not really God at all. He's not the author of evil but even evil must serve His ultimate purpose. Sin cannot exist outside of God's control or else God isn't truly sovereign.

I freely admit this is a mystery, but it is a mystery inherent in being creatures and not the Creator. The fact that we can't fully understand these things simply proves once again that "He is God and we are not." We do not choose God even though we may like to think that we do. Or if we do "choose" God, it's because He chose us first. God always has the first move. And in another realm of life, we do not choose our race or sex or culture or skin colour or our national origin. Those things come to us by virtue of our physical birth. They are part of who we are whether we like it or not.

The message is, stay the way God made you and stay in the place God put you. Be a Christian where you are right now. Evidently some of the Corinthians, having been converted out of idolatry, were jettisoning every part of their old life in favour of something radically different. The same thing often happens today. "I'm saved so I can quit my job." No! "I'm a Christian, I don't have to finish university." No! "I'm a Christian. I can move to the mountain and pray." No! "I'm a Christian. I don't have to obey the law anymore." No! Away with all such foolish talk! Nothing proves the reality of your conversion more than staying where you are and showing the change by the way you live. Don't cut and run. Stay where you are and live for Christ.

In order to help us understand this principle, Paul offers two examples.

The first is ***circumcision*** (1 Cor.7:18-19)

He basically says that circumcision doesn't matter one way or the other. If you are a Jew (and therefore circumcised), don't try to be uncircumcised once you come to Christ. If you are a Gentile (and therefore uncircumcised), don't think you need to be circumcised once you are saved. It doesn't matter one way or the other. That fact would not have bothered the Gentiles (who didn't care about circumcision anyway) but it would have hugely troubled the Jews who viewed circumcision as the visible mark of their covenant relationship with God. Paul just waves his hand, so to speak, and brushes away the whole controversy. Stay the way you are - circumcised or uncircumcised. It's not worth worrying about one way or the other.

The second example is more difficult because it involves *slavery* (1 Cor.7:21-23)
We have some trouble with this one, in part because we don't live in a society where slavery is a routine part of life. In the United Kingdom slavery was once legal, but that ended years ago. No one today has grown up in a world where slavery was common. By contrast, slavery was a major part of life in the Roman Empire. Experts tell us that there were perhaps 100 million slaves in the Roman Empire in the first century. That meant that in many cities, there were far more slaves than free people. Simple maths suggested that eventually many slaves would respond to the gospel and come into the church. What did the gospel have to say to their sad situation? Paul's advice sounds strange to us, and might today be called politically incorrect. In essence, he tells the slaves, don't worry about your slavery. Serve God where you are. In verse 21 he does say, if you can gain your freedom, do so. But that would not apply to most slaves. In those days a master occasionally freed his slaves, but that was unusual. And there was a way in which a slave could purchase his freedom, but it was expensive, took a long time, and was not practised everywhere.

The truth was very simple: If you were a slave, you were likely to stay a slave forever. That left only one question: Would you serve God in that disagreeable situation or would you focus so much on your slavery that you didn't serve God? Verse 22 says: "For he who was a slave when he was called by the Lord is the Lord's freedman; similarly, he who was a free man when he was called is Christ's slave." Paul's argument moves from the exterior to the interior. It's better to be a slave on the outside and a freeman in your heart because you know Jesus than to be free on the outside and enslaved to sin on the inside.

Knowing Jesus takes precedence over all outward circumstances. "You were bought at a price", he says in verse 23, referring to the blood of Jesus. If Jesus purchased you, then you are both free from sin and are now a servant of Christ.

The application could not be clearer. Don't let your slavery be an excuse not to serve the Lord. We can extrapolate from there to any extremely difficult circumstance of life. Many times we will find ourselves in places we would rather not be. Sometimes we are in those places for weeks or months or years or even for a lifetime. And we can't just push a button or say a prayer and make the difficulty go away. In those cases, we have to decide whether or not we will serve the Lord. Serve God where you are until God clearly calls you elsewhere. It's not wrong to better yourself but more money or a new position doesn't necessarily mean a better situation. Seek God first. That's the key to knowing God's will. If I'm going to live for God, I can do that at the factory, in the office, at the shop. I can do that while driving an old car or a newer model, or while living in a Victorian mansion or in a flat. I can serve God single or married. It doesn't matter. If I'm not going to live for God, I can be disobedient at the factory, in the office, at the shop, while driving an old car or a newer model, or while living in a Victorian mansion or in a flat. I can disobey God single or married. It doesn't matter. The issue is God - not my circumstances.

We like to say, "Change my circumstances and then I'll be happy." Paul says, "Get close to God and He will take care of your circumstances." So one man is a cook. Another is a cleaner. Another is a hospital porter. Another is a painter. Another is a banker. Another washes the sheets. Another keeps the lawn. Another tends the animals. Another serves the meals. Another prepares the food. And so it goes. What does it matter what we are called to do? It doesn't matter at all! All Christ's servants are honoured in His sight.

None of this is an argument against change per se. Like most people, I've moved from one job to another, from one church to another, from one location to another, and I've owned a series of cars. Change is inevitable in life but it's not a guaranteed solution to our problems. That fact leads us directly to the second important principle in this passage.

Two: Change is not wrong but it is not always an improvement.

The second principle comes from Paul's teaching in verses 25-28. Because of the "present crisis" he advises everyone to stay as they are. Evidently that phrase refers to some particular pressure on the church in Corinth. Because it was a cosmopolitan, seaport town, Corinth was known for a particularly immoral brand of idolatry. Converts to Christ faced enormous moral, spiritual and cultural pressure to compromise their faith. Perhaps there was a wave of local persecution that threatened the existence of the church. Although we don't know the particulars, Paul's advice is clear. Don't make any drastic changes. Stay as you are. When the seas are raging, it's not the right time to be changing ships. Stay the course! If you are married, stay married. If you are single, stay single.

Then he adds a very practical word: "But if you do marry, you have not sinned; and if a virgin marries, she has not sinned. But those who marry will face many troubles in this life, and I want to spare you this." The sense of the passage is clear. Stay as you are, especially if you are single. Don't feel it's necessary to be married. But if you desire to be married, you are not sinning. If you want to be married, and if you can find someone who wants to marry you (always a crucial requirement), and if both of you are believers in Christ, go ahead and get married. This is not wrong. But don't be so starry-eyed that you enter marriage with your eyes closed. As one man told me on the night I got married, "They say love is blind, but marriage is an eye-opener." He was right about that.

Don't think that marriage will make you happy and solve your problems. Don't think that marriage will bring you closer to God and make you a better person. It will not because it cannot. Marriage is good and noble and holy and honourable but it's not the be all and end all of life. If you are miserable being single, how can you be sure you'll suddenly be happy being married? The happiest married people are generally those who were also happy while being single. Changing your marital status doesn't guarantee a change in your happiness or your contentment or your satisfaction with life. Discontented singles aren't usually the best candidates for a happy marriage.

Three: Remember that you are a visitor on earth, not a permanent resident.

Notice the two key phrases that bracket verses 29 to 31:
1) The time is short.
2) The world is passing away.

The first phrase reminds us of the brevity of life. No one lives forever on planet earth. You may live 30 or 40 or 50 years. Who knows? You may live 80 or 90 years, but sooner or later you're going to die. And no matter how long you live, you're going to be dead a lot longer than you're going to be alive. If you doubt that, just check out the nearest cemetery. Every grave is proof that the time is short.

The second phrase comes from a Greek expression that means something like, "This world is but a shadow of reality." Everything we see is shadowy, and insubstantial. It's an Ecclesiastes-type idea: Vanity of vanities, all is vanity. The world itself is not made to last forever. If we didn't learn that seeing what terrorist bombers can do, what else will happen to make sure we get the point?

So, the time is short and the world is passing away. What follows from this truth? Matthew Henry says that we should live with "holy indifference" to the things of this world. Verses 29-31 of 1 Corinthians 7 flesh this out in five different ways:

1) ***With regard to our intimate relationships***: From now on those who have wives should live as if they had none." Now there's a verse you don't hear quoted at many weddings. It simply means, enjoy your marriage but don't make your marriage the most important thing in your life.
2) ***With regard to afflictions***: "Those who mourn, as if they did not."
3) ***With regard to pleasure***: "Those who are happy, as if they were not." He doesn't mean to suggest that we shouldn't weep or that we shouldn't rejoice and enjoy life, but he does mean that life is more than sorrow or joy. Perhaps we can say it this way. When a loved one dies, don't mourn so much that you make people think you don't believe in heaven. When you are having a good time, don't laugh so much that you make people think you don't believe in hell. In everything you do, don't forget about eternal realities.
4) ***With regard to employment***: "Those who buy something, as if it were not theirs to keep."
5) ***With regard to all earthly concerns***: "Those who use the things of the world, as if not engrossed in them."

Use and enjoy the world. Live and work in the world. Buy and sell in the world. But, but do not let the world rule your life. Be careful lest the things you possess end up possessing you. The message is clear and unmistakable. You won't be here forever. In all your living and going and doing and buying and selling, your giving and receiving, your singing and celebrating, during all of it, remember that you will not live forever. "Nothing golden lasts." Enjoy life, live it to the fullest measure, take advantage of every moment, but don't indulge yourself so much that you lose your focus on what really matters.

Writer and Pastor John Piper has exhorted the Christian community to adapt a "wartime mentality." He is referring to the rising clash of spiritual kingdoms around the world. These are awesome days for world evangelism, days in which the battle lines are being drawn in the sand, so to speak. Sooner or later, we'll all have to decide which side we are on. In times like these, Christians must be ready to engage in serious spiritual warfare.

So the message is, don't be preoccupied with things that don't matter. Figure out what matters in life - and then go and do it. As the old gospel song says, *"This world is not my home, I'm just a passin' through."* Don't try to hang on to the things of the world. That includes the dearest relationships of life. Ponder these sobering words of our Lord: "If anyone comes to me and does not hate his father and mother, his wife and children, his brothers and sisters - yes, even his own life - he cannot be my disciple. And anyone who does not carry his cross and follow me cannot be my disciple." Reading those verses, it's hard not to stumble at the word "hate" because to us, it implies some sort of hostility. The key rests in the phrase "even his own life." It must be something like this: Don't regard your life itself as something that must be preserved at all costs. Leave the future in God's hands. You may be called to do something that seems "reckless" for the sake of the Kingdom. Others will not understand and may even think you foolhardy. And the same is true for the closest relationships of life. Others may not understand and may even think you "hate" your own family. It's not true, of course, but it may seem that way because of your service for Christ.

In that light let's reconsider verse 29: "Those who have wives should live as if they had none." Widows know what this means. Live knowing that your marriage cannot last forever. Most likely, one of you will outlive the other. Live in the light of that day. Marriage is a temporary blessing at best. The same goes for child rearing. Many couples divorce when the children leave home because they built their lives around something that could not last. You came into the world single, you will go out single because your marriage ends the moment you die. Neither marriage nor children can give final meaning to your life. If you want this truth in one sentence, here it is: Hold lightly what you value greatly because you can't keep it forever anyway.

This week I was reminded again of the story of Jim Elliot. My daughter has been reading a new book about these events. In January 1956 five missionaries sought to bring the gospel to the Auca Indians of Ecuador. They were killed because the Indians feared the white men and thought they

61

had come to harm them. The missionaries knew the danger they were facing and took as many precautions as possible. But in the end they were killed, and from their death came a groundswell of young people volunteering for missionary service. In her book *Through Gates of Splendour,* Elizabeth Elliot tells of the frank discussions she and Jim had about the dangers of making the first face-to-face contact with the Aucas. At one point he said to her, "If it is the will of God, darling, I am ready to die for the salvation of the Aucas." Both sides of that prophetic statement came true. In the years to come, God used the death of those missionaries to bring many of the Aucas to faith in Christ.

"*Let goods and kindred go, this mortal life also,*
The body they may kill, God's truth abideth still,
His kingdom is forever."

Four: The most important thing is to give undivided devotion to the Lord.

This principle comes from verses 32-35 in 1 Corinthians 7 where Paul points out that singles have freedoms that those who are married don't have. Singles can serve the Lord without as many earthly distractions. Those who are married are divided in the sense that they must, and should, give attention to the needs of their spouses. It's only right that a husband should care about his wife, and it is natural and normal that a wife should concern herself with the needs of her husband. This is right and good, but the energy devoted to those worthy causes is time and effort that might have been devoted to the service of the Lord. To say it that way makes it sound as if Paul believes singleness is more righteous than marriage. or that marriage is less godly than being single. But that is not the case. You can serve the Lord effectively either way. But there is an undeniable truth in Paul's point. Certainly every married person knows that marriage is both a blessing and a heavy burden. Not an onerous burden, but a burden of care and concern, of time and money and prayers and thought and tears and love and energy.

To be truly married means giving of yourself unstintingly to the one you love. If you are single, that time and energy could be directly applied to the service of others in the name of Christ. This is Paul's point. He wishes us to understand that the greatest calling in life is serving the Lord with an undivided heart. Singles have an easier time of that if they will apply their hearts in the right direction.

To those reading this who are single, let me say: Use your time to serve the Lord. If you are young and unmarried, this is a message you especially need to hear. If you don't use your days to serve the Lord, you are wasting this part of your life. Don't spend your days pining away, dreaming about marriage and hoping against hope that the man or woman of your dreams will miraculously appear on a white horse to rescue you. Only God knows whether or not you will be married someday. Leave it in His hands. Don't spend your waking hours scheming about being married. Use your time and energy to serve the Lord. That doesn't mean it's wrong to want to be married, or to plan to be married, or to ask God for a marriage partner. Such thoughts are normal and good. But don't let those noble thoughts become the all-consuming passion of your life. Serve the Lord and let your future rest in His capable hands. If you are married, give thanks to God for your husband or wife. Love the mate God has given you. Pray for them. Look for ways to build them up spiritually. Let your marriage be part of your service for the Lord.

In conclusion

So the question comes down to this: Do you believe in God, or don't you? Do you believe God will give you what you need right now so you can serve Him right where you are? There is a sense in which, when you complain and dwell in discontentment, at that point you no longer believe in God. That is, on one level you certainly do believe in God, but by your discontented complaining, you are denying the truth you claim to believe. If you can't do everything you would like to do, you can joyfully accept your situation as being from the hand of the Lord. You can always pray, praise and sing in your heart to the Lord. You can always refresh yourself in the streams that flow forth from the heart of God.

Certain practical applications flow from all of this:
1) Bloom where you are planted.
2) Let God define your life, not earthly circumstances.
3) Don't expect change to make you happy.
4) Never forget that you won't be here forever.

The second of those four points seems most fundamental to me. We fall into a complaining spirit precisely because we have chosen to let our circumstances, including our relationships, define who we are. If we define ourselves first and foremost as being single, and if we desperately want to be married, it is quite likely that our self-definition will lead to discontentment. But if we decide to let God define who we are, then we can be in "good" or "bad" circumstances, as we all are sooner or later, and still find the contentment we seek.

The most practical application is this: Do God's will where you are and the rest will take care of itself. That doesn't mean you won't have hard decisions to make, and it doesn't mean that you won't slog through some very tough days, and it may mean that you face many months or years of adversity. But whether those hard times are short or long, our only recourse is to get up each day and do God's will the best we can do it on that particular day. If we do that, then tomorrow will take care of itself. God will see to that.

That brings us to a very important spiritual truth. The only thing that matters is knowing Jesus and through Him, growing closer to God day by day; nothing else matters. If we know God in Christ, then we are of all people most blessed and highly favoured. We have been blessed with every spiritual blessing in the heavenly places in Christ Jesus. If we don't know Christ, then the rest of life won't satisfy our deepest longings anyway. Christ must be the centre of life or else the circumference will never satisfy. Circumstances - even happy ones - can never replace the soul's longing for the Lord.

Seen in that light, discontentment is a grievous sin because it is an attempt to overthrow God. It is an attack on the Sovereign who sits on the throne of the universe. When you complain against the Lord, you are repeating Satan's mistake. It's the first great rebellion played out in your own heart, and you will not be any more successful than Lucifer was.

A great deal of our problem in this area stems from the fact that we don't really know who God is. Too many of us have a wrong view of God: Eager to make us happy, He adjusts His plans to fit our needs and lives to bring us to "self-actualisation" and personal fulfilment. It may surprise some people to discover that the biblical picture is quite different. With regard to His sovereignty, the God of the Bible is an autocrat; a divine despot who does whatever pleases Him. As the Creator, He has the final word regarding everything in the universe. We like to talk about the voice of the people, the will of the people, and how the majority rules. The universe is not a democracy, it's a theocracy: it's a divine monarchy. God doesn't give us the vote. He doesn't poll the universe to see what His next move should be. The Lord can say, "Come" and we come; "Go" and we go; "I need you there" and we must obey. We dare not fight back. We dare not murmur against the Master.

If we are truly surrendered to the Lord, and if we have any true concept of what "lordship" really means, this is what we should say: "Jesus Christ is my Lord. I will do what He says. He has the absolute right to my life. He has the unchallenged right to direct my affairs. He places me where He wants me. My response is unqualified, absolute, unquestioning submission."

That's what Paul means when he declares in Romans 14:8 that whether we live or die, we belong to the Lord. Once we understand this principle, our true position will become evident. Down on your faces before him! Bow down and worship the Lord. One of our beloved Christmas carols says, "O come, let us adore Him." And that is our calling and our proper response to the great truth of God's absolute sovereignty over all the details of life. The Magi understood the truth better than we do. The "Three Kings" brought their gifts to Jesus and then worshipped Him. It is not better to be a king than a shepherd because all stand on the same level ground before the Lord.

I close the chapter with this final thought: You were not made to be independent. You must serve someone. Make your choice. Jesus Christ bought you with His own blood. He gave everything to set you free from sin. Will you now serve Him? Or will you continue to complain? Yield yourself to Him completely. It is the only way to be free. As long as you demand your freedom to do whatever you want, you will always be in chains. "If the Son makes you free, you will be free indeed."

Chapter 5
Conquering Fear Of The Future

Newspaper headlines tell a chilling story: *"Riots... The High Cost of Peace... Thousands of Troops Needed.... Terrorism... Prepare For War... Perilous Times".*

The last headline is arresting, at least for those of us raised on the King James Bible, because it calls to mind a verse many of us heard (and memorised) years ago, "In the last days perilous times shall come." These are indeed "perilous times" in many ways. The clash between science and religion was supposed to be a defining characteristic of the modern age. But today's distinctive terror is modern science in the service of religious fanatics. The dangers in the Middle East. The reality of bio-terrorism.

This is a dangerous time to be alive, or more accurately, a dangerous time to try to stay alive. Yet life goes on, a bit uncertainly perhaps, but we all have our business to attend to. There are classes to teach, orders to fill, patients to see, books to write (and read), games to be played, and watched, papers to write, bills to pay, medicine to take, songs to sing, meals to prepare, and beyond that, there are the closer concerns of marriage and children and friends and family members. Many days it is easier to dismiss the larger concerns of the world in favour of wondering how you will spend the next few weeks.

A quick survey of what worries Churchgoers has revealed the following: *"Financial security. Health. Marriage. A place to live. Loneliness. Inability to get pregnant. Job loss."* Who among us could not relate to these concerns? These people are not unaware of what is happening in the world, but their deepest worries are closer to home.

Someone has said that worry is "the interest paid by those who borrow trouble." Another person called worry "a thin stream of fear trickling through the mind." Here in England, worry has become part of our national culture. You could write on countless gravestones the epitaph: *'Hurried, Worried, Buried.'*

Perhaps our greatest fear is the fear of death. Hebrews 2:15 tells us that Christ came to deliver those who had been enslaved by the fear of death all their lives. It's not just the fear of dying that troubles us; it's the thought of leaving this life with so much left to do. For some people both living and dying can seem equally painful.

The apostle Paul addresses the issue Romans 8. In verse 38 he writes, "I am convinced that neither death nor life... Paul adds all sorts of other scenarios of what can happen and finishes on this note... will not "be able to separate us from the love of God that is in Christ Jesus our Lord." Why is this the case? Because he has said in verse 37, "No, in all these things we are more than conquerors through Him who loved us."

With all that looms before us both internationally and personally, how can we move from fear to faith? In order to answer those questions, let's take a look at the story of a young woman named Esther. Even though the events took place almost 25 centuries ago, the story of her amazing courage points the way to a life free from consuming fear over what might happen tomorrow.

Learning from history.

The year was 465 B.C. A man named Xerxes was king of Persia. The most powerful man in the world, he ruled an empire even bigger than the empire of Nebuchadnezzar. His empire spread from India in the east to Greece in the west to Africa in the south to Turkey in the north. Our story takes place in one of his capital cities. In those days the Persian Empire had four capital cities. One you've heard of - Babylon. Another one called Ecbatana; one called Persepolis and yet a fourth one called Susa and it's there that our story unfolds.

It is fitting that we should consider a story that took place in Susa for it is not far from the centre of action in the Middle East today. In fact archaeologists dug up Susa about 100 years ago and found the ruins of the palace spoken of in the book of Esther. If you wanted to get to Susa, on a good day you could fly into Baghdad and get a bus out of the city and come south toward the mouth of the Persian Gulf. When you reach the mouth of the Persian Gulf you would turn left across the coastlands, cross the disputed border with Iran, and then you would make your way for another 100 miles. You would begin to come north again up into the Plain of Khuzistan and there, by the shores of the Karkheh River, you would see what would appear to be a large mound, flat on top, with some ruins above it. That's all that is left today of the ancient city of Susa. But in 465 B.C., Susa was one of the world's greatest cities. Darius the Mede, father of King Xerxes, built his winter palace there. Archaeologists discovered a tablet in the ruins that describes how he built the city of Susa. He imported cedar from Lebanon, hardwood from Gandara, gold from Sardis, lapis lazuli from Sogdiana, ebony and silver from Egypt, ivory from Ethiopia and turquoise from Chorsmia.

After the death of Darius, Xerxes continued the work his father had begun. The real capital was in Babylon. Susa served as the winter palace. It was a place to get away from the pressures of Babylon. The king of Persia kept his harem in Susa. The harem was a large group of beautiful women who were there at his beck and call to serve him in any way he wished. They were gathered from among the most beautiful women in the empire - both Persian women and women from foreign countries. They had been given a special diet and taught a special way of life and their only calling was to please the king. One after another he would call the women in and they would serve him and do his bidding.

In the course of time the king, who had become enraged at Queen Vashti for some indiscretions, began to search out his harem to find the most beautiful, most attractive, most desirable woman so that he might make her the new queen. As he searched through the harem in Susa, one after another, he looked at one woman after another. But he could not find what he wanted until at last he came upon a woman whose beauty, character, form and comeliness was such that he was completely taken with her. He said, "I want her to be my queen." Her name in Hebrew was Hadassah, and in Persian, Esther. She was a Jew, one of God's chosen people and without any forewarning, she suddenly becomes the Queen of Persia. She is now the most important woman in the entire realm - a Jewish woman, queen to a Persian king.

Life was good for Esther because she was the king's chosen one. She was the one on whom his favour rested. For many days, months and years Esther basked in the glory of being the chief woman of the realm and the one to whom everyone else bowed and paid homage.

Then a crisis hit! A certain man named Haman came in to see the king. Esther knew nothing about it because in those days the king kept his business and his women far apart. So while Esther was with the other women, the king saw Haman. Haman came in with a story the king could hardly believe. He said, "Oh, king, there's a certain people in your realm who are treasonous and seditious against you. They do not follow your law. They do not pay homage to you. They do not respect what you have done. O king, we must do something about these people." Haman neglected to tell the king that he was talking about the Jews. As a matter of fact, the things he was saying were not true. The Jews were not all bad. They were not treasonous. But Haman, because he was a descendant of the Amalekites, the ancient enemies of the people of God, wanted to stir up trouble against the Jews.

So he said to the king, "We must do something about these people who are polluting your kingdom." The king asked, "What do you propose?" And Haman answered, "If you will allow me, I will write a decree and have you sign it with your signet ring and we will send a decree out over all the kingdom. The decree will be that on a certain day all the Jews will be put to death." This is called a pogrom. It is an ancient version of what the Nazis did in World War II.

Haman's idea was to kill all the Jews in the Persian Empire on the same day.

Don't miss this one fact. Haman did not tell the king that he was talking about the Jews so the king didn't know. Not that it would have made that much difference to a Persian king anyway. So the decree was signed and sealed with the signet ring and it began to go out over all the land.

Enter a man by the name of Mordecai, cousin to Queen Esther. He was a Jew serving in the court of King Xerxes. As a cabinet officer, he was deeply involved in the business affairs of the king, a man of good character, a man whom the king greatly respected. When Mordecai heard what Haman had done, which would mean that he and all his relatives would be put to death, he went to the middle of the city and clothed himself with sackcloth and ashes and began mourning and wailing.

Word of what Mordecai had done reached the ears of Queen Esther. She had not heard about Haman's wicked plot and when she heard that Mordecai was in mourning, she sent her messenger to find out what had happened. He gave the messenger a copy of the decree and said, "Go back to the queen and tell her that she is the only one who can save us now. If she does not act we will all die." We pick up the story in Esther 4:9 to 11.

Fear strikes

Hathach, the messenger from Esther, went back and reported to Esther what Mordecai had said. Then she instructed him to say to Mordecai, "All the king's officials and the people of the royal provinces know that for any man or woman who approaches the king in the inner court without being summoned the king has but one law: that he be put to death."

All the monarchs of the ancient Near East were absolute despots. You did not come near them without an invitation. If a man rushed in to see the king and the king was startled and didn't want to see him, without a word the man would be taken out and put to death, so you had to think and think again before you went in to see the king. "The only exception to this is for the king to extend the gold sceptre to him and spare his life. But thirty days have passed since I was called to go to the king" says Esther.

It's hard for us to understand that today but you must remember this is an ancient Near East nation where even though she was the queen, she was still part of the harem. During the thirty days the king had not seen Esther, Mordecai is saying, "Esther, you've got to save us." Esther is saying, "Mordecai, you don't understand what you're asking me to do."

She's not refusing, you understand. She's not saying, "No, I won't do it." She's just saying, "Before you ask me to do that, you've got to understand what the risk is. If I go in there and the king doesn't want to see me, I will be put to death even though I am the queen. Mordecai, think about what you are asking me to do." She wasn't saying no. She was doing what any reasonable individual would do. She was counting the personal cost.

That's always true any time we're called to get involved. Anytime the phone rings, anytime there's an appeal, anytime there's a great cause put before us, anytime the challenge is great, you have to consider what is involved. Before you take the first step you had better sit down and count the personal cost. That's a biblical thing to do. Nobody goes to war without counting the soldiers to make sure he's got enough. Nobody sits down to build a building without making sure he has enough money to finish the job. If you want to be my disciple, Jesus said, you must take up your cross and follow me. It's going to cost you something.

So Esther is saying, "Mordecai, I want to help you but you've got to understand something. I am taking my life in my hands if I'm going to get involved with you." She was the queen. She had a good life. She had anything she wanted. She would raise her hand and fifty servants would come to her. Just say the word and whatever she wanted was given to her. All those other women would have given anything to be in her position. She had it all: material wealth, fame, popularity, adulation, the approval of her friends. Now Mordecai is saying "Esther, it's time for you to put it all on the line."

The messenger goes back and tells Mordecai what Esther had said. Mordecai's answer is the heart of the book of Esther. When Esther's words were reported to Mordecai, he sent back this answer, "Do not think that because you are in the king's house you alone of all the Jews will escape. For if you remain silent at this time, relief and deliverance for the Jews will arise from another place, but you and your father's family will perish. And who knows but that you have come to royal position for such a time as this?" He makes three appeals to her.

Responsibility calls

Mordecai appeals to her. He says, "Esther, you're the queen, but underneath all that queenly regalia beats a Jewish heart. You're one of God's people. Don't think by remaining silent you can avoid persecution, because you can't. Once the killing starts it's going to be mighty hard to stop. Once the crowds start killing the Jews one by one, they'll start with the common people but, Esther, they'll wind up on your doorstep and they won't stop killing until they've killed all the Jews including you and your family. Don't think that your position or privilege exempts you from what is going to happen. Just because you're the queen, you are not out of trouble. You may be the last to go, but you're going to go."

We should learn from this that there is no safety in this world, not even for the rich and powerful. After terrorism on our streets we ought to be fully convinced of this fact. Riches cannot save you from the troubles of the world. Then he said, "If you don't help us" - if you do remain silent - "relief and deliverance will arise from another place." This is one of the most amazing statements in all of the Old Testament. It is certainly the most amazing statement in the book of Esther.

Let me share a piece of Bible trivia with you. Did you know that Esther is the only book in the Bible in which the name of God is not directly mentioned? You will never find the words "God" or "Lord" in the Book of Esther. That's one of the reasons some people have looked at the Book of Esther and have concluded that it's not important or not inspired or doesn't belong in the Bible or isn't worthy of our close study. But I'll tell you why the name of God is not in there. It's because the book of Esther is the story of God's people in a foreign land. It's the story of God's people under Gentile domination. It is a real story that serves as a kind of parable to teach us a lesson about how God works through seemingly unconnected circumstances to deliver His people even when they are under Gentile domination. That is why the name God never appears.

Esther believed in God. So did Mordecai. So did all the Jews. That's what made them Jews - they believed in God. But His name is never mentioned because it's a lesson about the providence and liberating power of God. So Mordecai is saying, "If you don't help us, God is able to help us from some other source but you yourself will be destroyed." Then he says, "Who knows but that you have come to royal position for such a time as this?"

Ponder those words for a moment. "Esther, don't forget where you came from. There was a time when you were lined up with all those other women in the harem. You ate at the same table with them. You dressed the same way they dress. You acted just like them. Nobody knew you were a Jew. Esther, what made the king pick you out? Did you think it was just your good looks? They were all good looking. Do you think it was just your smile? They could all smile. Do you think it was just the way you flirted? They could all flirt."

Mordecai's message is crystal-clear: "Esther, you're sitting here and you're the queen. You've got it all. You're on top. You've got privilege beyond anyone else in the whole kingdom. Do you think that happened by chance? Do you think that's coincidence? Esther, the reason you're on top is because God put you there. Do you know why God put you there? He put you there so that at the crucial moment of history you could say the word and you could deliver your people. All of that training and all you went through, it happened so that you would be the instrument God would use to deliver his people." What a view of history this is.

It's an important way of looking at the circumstances of life. What a way of understanding the work of God. "Esther, who knows but that you have come to royal position for such a time as this?" For this critical moment. For this one moment in history. "Who knows, Esther, but that you have come here for this one thing? All that's happened to you is preparation for this moment."

Trust wins

We read Esther's response in verses 15 and 16. Then Esther sent this reply to Mordecai: "Go, gather together all the Jews who are in Susa, and fast for me. Do not eat or drink for three days, night or day. I and my maids will fast just as you do. When this is done, I will go to the king, even though it is against the law. And if I perish, I perish."

Do you get the principle here? Mordecai's great appeal to Esther was based on a great principle. The greater the privilege, the greater the responsibility. The more you have, the more you have to answer for. The more God has given you, the greater your responsibility to use it for His Kingdom. What does this ancient story teach us about overcoming our own fear of the future?

For one thing, we learn that there is no safety in the world. Bad things happen to good people all the time. Sometimes they appear to be "random" acts of tragedy, and sometimes, evil people conspire against us.

We also learn that there are no coincidences in life. You are where you are because God wants you to be there. You probably aren't a queen in a foreign court, but wherever you are right now, God had a hand in getting you there. And your highest calling is to use your position in life to support the cause of Christ in the world.

75

In the end we must do what Esther did - fast and pray and seek the Lord so that when the time comes, we can do the right thing, the hard thing, the tough choice that lies along the road of obedience to God, leaving the results with Him.

That's the real meaning of, "If I perish, I perish." Those are solemn words of faith spoken by a woman who has put her life in God's hands. As I thought about her courage, the Lord put this insight on my heart: There is no one so free as the person who is not afraid to die. If you aren't afraid to die, then you are free to serve the Lord and do whatever He calls you to do.

If you know the Lord, then you don't have to fear death. If you don't fear death, you're truly free and the devil has lost his greatest weapon against you.

Looking to the future.

As we look ahead to the weeks that stretch before us, here are four truths that ought to encourage us:

1) God is already there because He is the God who goes before His people.
2) God promises to be with you no matter what happens to you.
3) If you know the Lord, the worst thing that can happen is that you will go to heaven earlier than you expected, which is also the best thing that can happen to you.
4) You will have all the time you need to do everything God wants you to do.

In some ways, that last point is the most important one because many of us go into a new week feeling a bit harassed and hurried. No matter what else happens in the next few months, rest assured that you will have all the time, all the strength, and all the wisdom you need to do everything God wants you to do.

That principle should not be stretched to mean that you are guaranteed to accomplish all your goals or that every one of your dreams will come true. We still live in a fallen world where things break down and nothing works quite right. But given that limitation, we can have confidence that God will supply all that we truly need, when we need it, so that we can do his will. No one can say with certainty what the next few months will bring. None of us knows if we will even be here twelve months from now. But that thought should not alarm us in any way. To all our fears the Lord says quite simply: "Fear not."

> Will things get worse?
> Will I lose my health?
> Will I get cancer?
> Will I keep my job?
> Will my loved ones struggle?
> Will my investments collapse?
> Will I run out of money this year?
> Will tragedy strike in my family?
> Will my children disappoint me?
> Will others ridicule my faith?
> Will my plans come to nothing?
> Will my dreams turn to ashes?
> Will I face death this year?

Fear Not!

Things we don't want to happen may happen, and sooner than we think. Indeed, some of them are bound to happen to us eventually. But the word of the Lord remains. *Fear not.* The Lord himself is with us today and He will be with us tomorrow. We of all people ought to be optimistic as we face the future. We have a great future because we have a great God. So chin up, child of God. Stop staring in the soup. Pull those shoulders back. Put a smile on your face. Take your troubles, wrap them up, and give them all to the Lord. We'll have our share of hard times, but overriding it all is the promise of God who said, "I will never leave you or forsake you."

On Christmas Day 1939, King George VI gave a brief radio address to his troubled nation. We were already at war with Germany. Soon all of Europe would be plunged into the horror of brutal, unrestrained warfare. Hoping to calm the troubled hearts of his countrymen, the king offered words of encouragement as the storm clouds gathered overhead. He ended his remarks by quoting a hitherto unknown poem by Louise Haskins, "The Gate of the Year." It has since become known around the world:

> *"I said to the man who stood at the gate of the year:*
> *'Give me a light, that I may tread safely into the unknown!'*
> *And he replied:*
> *'Go out into the darkness and put your hand into the Hand of God.*
> *That shall be to you better than light and safer than a known way.'"*

What a word that is for us today. No one but God knows what the future holds. Let us do as the poet suggested and place our hands in the hand of Almighty God, and let us go out into the unknown future with confidence, knowing that if God goes with us, we need not fear the future. To walk with the Lord is the greatest of all joys, and it is indeed safer than a known way.

PART TWO

COMBATING...

Chapter 6
God Cares About Our Anxiety!

Death was walking into a city. *Life* asked, "Where are you going?" "To claim 10,000 people by night fall", replied *Death*. "That's awful." "It's my job", said *Death*. Later that evening *Death* was seen walking out of the city." *Life* saw him and said, "You lied. You said that you would claim 10,000 people but 20,000 died today." *Death* replied, "I did only claim 10,000. Worry and anxiety killed the rest."

In terms of technology we have an easier life than any previous generation. And yet there is more uneasiness than ever before. I want to assure you God cares, and He has some profound words to say to you. They are found in 1 Peter 5:6-7, "Humble yourselves, therefore, under God's mighty hand, that He may lift you up in due time. Cast all your anxiety on Him for He cares for you." Verse 7 is such a powerful statement it cannot be ignored. It has only eleven words, and ten of them are one-syllable words – only the word "anxiety" has more than a single syllable. It's a simple verse, but carries a profound message. It's a message this stressed-out generation needs to hear.

A lot of us are suffering from emotional overload. Have you ever felt the same way David did when he wrote these words? "My pain has overwhelmed me like a burden too heavy to bear." You may be thinking, "I'm having to carry more than I can bear." I want to share with you how to unload your burdens.

The Bible word for anxiety means *"to divide"* or *"to distract."* Anxiety is having a disturbed and distracted mind. It's a fear or dread about some real or perceived threat. This definition of anxiety isn't from a medical journal, but it describes anxiety in a way most can understand: Anxiety is a gnawing dread in your gut that something bad may happen. Some of the visible symptoms of anxiety are restlessness, irritability, fatigue, difficulty in concentrating, and difficulty sleeping.

In the Bible, Job was a man who suffered severe anxiety. In a single day he lost his fortune, family, and his health. This is how he described his feeling of anxiety: "The churning inside me never stops; days of suffering confront me." If Job had known in the end God was going to reward his faithfulness with twice as much wealth, and another house full of children, that inner churning wouldn't have been as difficult to handle.

Our culture is experiencing an infectious anxiety epidemic. But medical studies have shown much of what we worry about constitutes needless anxiety. Studies reveal 40 percent of what we worry about will never happen. 30 percent of what we worry about is from the past and can't be changed. 12 percent is worry about criticism from others, much of it untrue. 10 percent of the things we worry about are health issues, which actually are worse when we worry. And only 8 percent of what we worry about constitutes real problems we have to face. So, 92 percent of your anxiety is needless. And the Bible says we are to cast 100 percent of our anxiety on God! I had to smile when someone said, "Don't tell me worry doesn't do any good. When I really worry about something, it doesn't happen."

Consider what anxiety does to us. It doesn't empty tomorrow of its sorrows but today of it's strength. It doesn't allow you to escape trouble but it does make you unfit to cope when the trouble comes. Anxiety is like a rocking chair. It will give you something to do but you're going nowhere with it!

Let me make a confession to you. Right now I'm worried! But what I'm worried about is that I will pile guilt on you by telling you not to worry. We need something more helpful than that – and we have it! People were anxious in the time of Jesus, too. Even people who knew Him personally suffered from worry. Jesus once visited the home of Mary and Martha for a meal. Because of the heat, many meals were eaten outdoors in a shaded atrium. Imagine Jesus is talking to Mary, sitting at His feet, just enjoying their conversation. We often assume Jesus was doing all the talking - like giving a sermon on the porch or something. But having been a husband for a long time, I suspect Mary was talking at least as much to Jesus - probably more. She was sharing her thoughts, her feelings, and her pain. Martha just explodes at this. She said to Jesus: *"Lord don't you care* that my sister has left me to do the work by myself? Tell her to help me!"* Freeze frame those four words for a minute: *'Lord, don't you care?'* Have you ever said or thought those exact words? I know I have. "Lord, I'm hurting here. Things are tough. It's as if you have your back turned to me. Lord, don't you even care?" But Jesus does care. He replied to Mary in words that contained both the diagnosis and the prescription for anxiety: "Martha, Martha, (repeating someone's name was a sign of affection) you are worried (the same word in 1 Peter 5:7 - a distracted, dreading attitude) Jesus continued, "You are upset about many things, but only one thing is needed. Mary has chosen what is better, and it will not be taken from her."

The one thing I need when I'm full of anxiety and upset about many things is to fall at the feet of Jesus and cast my cares and anxiety on Him. Let me underline that - When I'm full of worry and upset about many things I need to get on my knees and give my anxiety to Jesus, because He cares for me!"

1 Peter 5:7 spells it out: "Cast all your anxiety on Him because He cares for you." Notice two important truths in this verse.

(1) GOD'S PROPOSAL.

"Cast all your anxiety on Him". We try to carry our own burdens, but God invites us to cast them on Him. It's easier said than done. I can personally relate to the little poem that says:

> *It is His will that I should cast*
> *My care on Him each day.*
> *He also bids me not to cast*
> *My confidence away.*
> *But oh, how foolishly I act*
> *When taken unaware;*
> *I cast away my confidence*
> *And carry all my care!*

Think about that word *'cast'*. 'The Greek word for *cast* means *"to toss or to throw"*. The disciples of Jesus threw their cloaks onto the back of a borrowed colt for Jesus to ride into Jerusalem. It's the same word that's used here. Casting your anxiety on the Lord is like putting a saddle on a horse before you ride it. It would be preposterous for you to ride a horse while carrying the saddle on your shoulders. But that's what many of you are doing today with your problems - you're trying to carry them yourself instead of tossing them on the Lord.

Let's get a handle on how we do that. How do we cast cares, or throw them on the Lord? Do you know this little ditty?

> *"I've joined the new 'Don't Worry' club*
> *And now I hold my breath.*
> *I'm scared I'm going to worry,*
> *So I'm frightened half to death."*

Will-power alone won't get us free from anxiety or worry. Let me say something important in this regard. There is a difference between a problem and a fact. God doesn't deal with problems He deals with facts. Dogs bark, that's not a problem that's a fact. Cats meow, that's not a problem that's a fact. Leaves fall from trees in Autumn, it's not a problem it's a fact. You have a health problem – what can you do about it? Do it and work it down to a fact then give it to God. You have a money problem – what can you do about it? Do it and work it down to a fact then give it to God. You have a relationship problem – do what you can and then give it to God. Where we are anxious we must confront the problem and always work it down to a fact we then give it to God.

Golfers talk about 'learning on the other guys ball." In other words seeing the flight of his ball and reading it for your own attempt. If you want to learn how to do something well, you should seek out someone who is already doing it well and let them teach you. The Apostle Paul was an expert at casting his anxiety on the Lord. He had been stoned, shipwrecked, and beaten with sticks. He had plenty to worry about but he refused to be anxious. When he was in prison he wrote to teach us how to cast our anxiety on the Lord: "Don't fret or worry. Instead of worrying, pray. Let petitions and praises shape your worries into prayers, letting God know your concerns. Before you know it, a sense of God's wholeness will come and settle you down. It's wonderful what happens when Christ displaces worry at the centre of your life."

When you are worrying about something, you can't be praying about it. But when you are praying about something you can't be worrying about it. Too many Christians make the mistake of getting on their knees and telling God about their problems; then they get up and keep on carrying the burden themselves. Like the old song says, *"Take your burdens to the Lord and leave them there."*

There's a short story called "The Trouble Tree" (Author Unknown). I'll tell it in the first person voice of the writer.

Some years ago I hired a local carpenter to restore this old cabin. When he arrived he was frustrated because a traffic jam had made him late. The day only got worse. Some of the building material I had ordered never arrived, and then the motor in his electric saw burned out. Then, when he got ready to go home, his truck wouldn't start. So, he was pretty upset when I offered to drive him home, but he accepted my offer. I could still hear the traces of anger in his voice as he talked about the job. When we arrived he thanked me for the ride and invited me to meet his family. Just before he walked into his little house, he stepped over to a small tree and paused for a minute. He took his strong hands and touched the tips of several of the branches. As he opened the back door an amazing transformation occurred. A smile split his tanned face as he hugged his two daughters and wife, then as if he didn't have a care in the world he introduced me to his family. As he walked me back to my car I pointed to the tree and asked him about it. He said, "Oh, that's my trouble tree. It's not usual for me to have the kind of frustrating trouble I experienced today, but one thing's for sure, those troubles from the job don't belong in the house with my wife and girls. So every afternoon I just hang my troubles on this tree and then I pick 'em back up the next morning when I leave for work." He smiled and said, "It's a funny thing, though. When I come out in the morning to pick 'em up, there ain't nearly as many as I remember hanging there the night before - and they ain't nearly as heavy as they was yesterday."

Wouldn't it be great if you had a trouble tree? We've got something, or actually, *Someone* much better than a trouble tree. Jesus Christ hung on His very own trouble tree at Calvary. He did that because He cares for you. He cares for you so much He invites you to cast all your anxiety on Him.

In her book, *You Can Too,* Christian businesswoman Mary Crowley writes about how she learned to cast her anxiety on the Lord. She wrote: "When things go wrong, I just don't go with them. Every evening I turn my worries over to God. He's going to be up all night anyway."

Our *problem* is anxiety. God's *proposal* is to cast all our anxiety on Him, now consider . . .

(2) GOD'S PROMISE.

"He cares for you." There are hundreds of promises in the Bible that assure us God really does care for you and for me. I want to share just a few statements about God's character to prove just how much He cares for you. For those of you who like English grammar, these for statements are similes. A simile is a figure of speech in which two essentially different things are compared - often using the words 'as' or 'like'. If you remove the first 'I' in the word 'simile', you're left with the word 'smile'. It's true in the Christian life also that whenever you remove your ego, (the big 'I' who tries to be first) you'll smile at the result. A smile takes 17 muscles, a frown takes 43. You really are making your face work harder with a frown! Christians have more to smile about than anybody else. Each one of these similes about God should make you smile:

First: God cares for you like a daddy counting his child's first steps.

I remember how exciting it was when my baby girls took their first steps. One, two, three steps on her own. We were so excited! And then in a flash it seemed as if she had her driver's license and she was gone! Parents, do you remember how excited you were when your baby took those first steps? You probably called the grandparents and said, "John took four steps today." But you probably stopped counting the steps and started trying to chase them down!

God is like that. He counts your steps, and He never stops counting. The Bible says: "For what is man's lot from God above, his heritage from the Almighty on high? Does he not see my ways and count my every step?"... "Surely then, you count my steps but do not keep track of my sin." Isn't that wonderful? God counts our steps, but He doesn't keep track of the times we fall. You've already taken many steps, and perhaps you have many more steps to take - rest assured that God is watching and counting your every step. Your steps may lead you into a hospital room where you sit by the side of a suffering loved one - God counts those steps. Your steps may take you into a funeral home to look at the human remains of someone you loved - He counts those steps. Your steps may take you through divorce, disaster, and despair - God's counting them.

Few people work harder than birds. But they don't worry, they sing!

> "Said the Robin to the Sparrow,
> I should really like to know,
> Why these anxious human beings rush and worry so.
> Said the Sparrow to the Robin,
> Friend, I think that it must be,
> That they have no Heavenly Father,
> Such as cares for you and me."

Who cares? God cares for you, like a father counting his child's first steps!

Second: God cares for you like a mother calming her hurting child.

Every mother has an instinctive desire to protect her children from danger and to comfort them when they're hurting. A mother's touch and voice can soothe a troubled child like nothing else. Mothers also want their children to be happy. You might not remember it, but there was probably a time when your mother bounced you on her knee and chanted,

"Ride a little horsy, down to town;
Watch out baby, or you'll fall down!"

Did you know the Bible says God cares for you like a mother bouncing her child on her knee? In Isaiah 66 God says, "I will extend peace to her like a river, and the wealth of nations like a flooding stream; you will nurse and be carried on her arm and dandled on her knees. As a mother comforts her child, so will I comfort you".

We all know the Bible teaches God is our Heavenly Father, but did you know God reveals He relates to us as a mother as well? If you're a mum, I think you'll agree that there is an amazing connection between a mother and a baby. It goes deeper than just a physical relationship. A psychology professor conducted a test to determine this mother/child connection at a university hospital. Forty six mothers who gave birth in the previous five to seventy hours participated. Each mother was blindfolded and asked to identify which of three sleeping babies was hers. They were not told in advance, so they couldn't prepare by studying their child. In this test nearly 70 percent of the mothers correctly identified their babies. This mysterious connection between a mother and her baby is profound. Now multiply that connection a trillion times and you will begin to grasp how much God cares for you. He created you in love so you could be His child. Who cares? God cares for you like a mother comforting her hurting child!

Third: God cares for you like a hen covering her frightened chicks.

Of all of God's creatures, the hen is one of the most protective of her young. The Bible affirms that God will "cover you with His feathers, and under His wings you will find refuge."

Before His arrest and crucifixion, Jesus walked down the Mount of Olives and as He surveyed the panorama of the city of Jerusalem, He wept because the people rejected His offer of love and forgiveness. Today there is a chapel in that very spot on the Mount of Olives called the Chapel of Tears. Inside you can find a mosaic of a hen protecting her chicks. Jesus said, "How often I have longed to gather your children together, as a hen gathers her chicks under her wings, but you were not willing!"

A forest fire burnt down a farmhouse. As the embers cooled, the devastated farmer was walking over the ruins and noticed a burned lump on the ground. He prodded it with his stick and saw it was a hen, burned to death. The farmer turned the hen over and, to his surprise out ran three chirping baby chicks. The hen died in the flames even as it saved the lives of her helpless chicks. Jesus loves us so much He was willing to cover our sinfulness and to die so we can live. Who cares? God cares for you... like a hen covering her frightened chicks.

Fourth: God cares for you like an eagle coaxing its young to fly.

While you may not think a little hen is a noble analogy for God, you must admit that a soaring eagle is the most majestic of all the birds in God's creation. The Bible says, "Like an eagle that stirs up its nest and hovers over its young, that spreads its wings to catch them and carries them on its pinions. The Lord alone led him (Jacob)." The parent Golden Eagles teach their young to fly in a very unusual way. For the first ten weeks of their lives, an eaglet is safe and secure in its nest. The parent eagles protect and feed their young. A baby eagle doesn't fly instinctively, they have to be taught. At first they resist flying - who could blame them? They have a comfort zone in the nest! So the parents have to force their newborn eaglets to fly. They literally kick them out of the nest. First, they use their talons to stir up the nest. They expose the sharp ends of the sticks so that the eaglets are no longer in a comfort zone. Then the parent eagle flaps its wings furiously until the eaglets jump to the edge of the nest. Then the parent eagle pushes a single eaglet out and it falls, screeching as it plummets down. If the eaglet spreads its wings and catches the airflow, he may fly on the first try, but that seldom happens. If the eaglet doesn't fly, the parent eagle that has been falling with its young spreads its wings and flies under the eaglet. The eagle catches the eaglet and carries it on its pinions back to the nest. Then the process is repeated until each eaglet learns to fly. The behaviour of the parents may seem harsh, because some eaglets die learning to fly. But it is the desire of the parent eagles that their young spread their wings and soar into the sky.

What a great lesson for us! Some of you may think God is harsh toward you right now because He's stirred up your nest. Maybe God knows you've been stuck in your comfort zone too long. God loves you so much He is stirring up your life and He may be getting ready to push you out of your nest of complacency. Or you may have already been pushed out and it seems as if you're plummeting toward a hard landing. Don't worry God will be there to catch you. It may be terrifying at first, but God knows what He's doing. Who cares? God cares - like an eagle coaxing its young to fly.

Anxiety over your problems can be like bricks weighing you down. Life is full of these heavy bricks of adversity. Your bricks may be money, or health, or career, or school, or terrorism, or marriage, or children, or parents, or retirement, or even death - the ultimate anxiety. Imagine you are carrying these bricks of anxiety around in a backpack. It's going to make you miserable. And the whole time, Jesus is there, holding out His strong arms inviting you to cast all those anxieties on Him. While you're walking around bent over with the cares of the world, you need to hear the encouraging words of a great old hymn.

A neighbour sat with a very ill man. Looking at a manuscript at the bedside he discovered that the ill man had written the following words for his mother when she was going through a special sorrow.

This is what Joseph Scriven wrote:

> *"What a friend we have in Jesus!*
> *All our sins and griefs to bear.*
> *What a privilege to carry–*
> *everything to God in prayer.*
>
> *Oh, what peace we often forfeit,*
> *Oh, what needless pain we bear.*
> *All because we do not carry*
> *everything to God in prayer.*
>
> *Are we weak and heavy laden?*
> *Cumbered with a load of care?*
> *Precious Saviour still our refuge.*
> *Take it to the Lord in prayer.*
>
> *Can we find a friend so faithful,*
> *who will all our sorrows share?*
> *Jesus knows our every weakness.*
> *Take it to the Lord in prayer."*

When you stop trying to carry the weight of your problems and cast them into His arms, then you can experience the freedom and lightness of having a tremendous burden lifted off your shoulders.

Chapter 7
Happy Ever After!

"To boldly go where no man has gone before." Recognise that famous line? Here is a little trivia test. If you do recognise it, then somewhere along the way, you've been exposed to that cultural phenomenon known as *Star Trek.* You know at least a little about the "voyages of the Starship Enterprise." They had this invention on the Enterprise, you remember, it's called a *transporter* - as in "Scotty, beam me up!" (Yes I know those words were never actually said – but something like it was). The *transporter* sort of rearranges your molecules and beams you to another location almost immediately. But sometimes the crew would get beamed down to some unknown planet, only to be greeted by this horrific space creature. That's when it's time for "Beam me up!"

It's not always a good thing to be transported to another place, especially if there's something there you're not ready to handle. There is a *transporter* that sends your mind and your emotions right into tomorrow, before you're ready to handle tomorrow. This dangerous *transporter* has got a name. It's called *Worry*. In this chapter we continue to check the biblical principles about combating worry.

Recently I made a list of things to worry about. These things are not personal rather they touch on national and international issues that affect all of us. No one can say with certainty what will happen with all the wars and terrorist threats around the world. There is economic uncertainty. More important to you, I guess, there are personal crises and problems for which you may see no easy solution. You may not be worried about international problems. You have your own issues that keep you awake late into the night. Often we say *"Have a good day"* rather glibly - many times without any thought at all. Perhaps we should make it a question - *Will today be a good day for me?*

Instability is nothing new for the people of God. In every generation believers have faced moments when fear threatened to overwhelm faith. God's word to His people is always "Fear not." Years ago I remember reading that the phrase "Fear not" is repeated 366 times in the Bible - once for every day in the year and an extra one for leap year. I've never checked but I do know that God keeps saying it because it's a problem to us. No matter what happens this week, next week, next month - or in the years to come - God's word to you is the same: "Fear not."

Philippians 4:10-13 is perhaps the greatest statement in the New Testament on the subject of Christian contentment. We need to hear God's message to us in the midst of so much public and private uncertainty. I'd like to begin by offering my own three-part definition of contentment:

1) Contentment is the belief that I have everything I need at this present moment.
2) It is also the confidence that if I needed anything else, God would give it to me.
3) It is also the certainty that when I need anything else, God will give it to me.

The first part is the key. True contentment means understanding that, at any given moment, I have everything I truly *need.* I almost certainly don't have everything I *want.* And I probably don't have everything I *think* I need. This part of the definition means that God has so ordered the universe that no matter where you are right now you have everything you truly *need* to be content. That's an awesome statement - and I know it's one thing to say that when all is going well for you, it's something else to believe that when your husband walks out on you or the doctor says, "I'm sorry, there's nothing else we can do."

This raises a big question. We must ask: *How do we know this is true?* We know it because God has said it is true. He has promised to supply our needs. He has guaranteed that He will feed and clothe us. He has promised to hear our prayers. He has given the Holy Spirit to lead us and the

Word of God to guide us. He has redeemed us from our sins, given us new life, placed us in Christ, endowed us with every spiritual blessing in the heavenly places, seated us with Christ in heaven, given us abundant life, filled us with His Spirit, placed us in the body of Christ, promised us a way of escape in the moment of temptation, sent His angels to encamp around us, translated us from the realm of darkness into the kingdom of His dear Son, sealed us with the Spirit who is the earnest of our salvation, caused us to pass from death to life, justified us while we were still ungodly, called us His children, caused us to be born again by the Spirit, adopted us into His family, sanctified us, promised never to leave us, set our feet on the road to heaven, broken Satan's power, removed the fear of death, and guaranteed our future resurrection.

If all that is true, how can we doubt that God will give us what we need when we need it? And if we truly need something else, He'll give that to us too. Which means that if we don't have something we think we need, it's because our heavenly Father knows best and has chosen not to give it to us right now. If we truly need it later, He'll see that we get it. That applies to every area of life - to your finances, your job, your health, your marriage, your friendships, your children, your parents, every relationship of life, and to all your dreams for the future. You've got everything you need to be content right now - and if you're not, please don't blame God. It's not His fault.

Let's take a look and see how this principle works out in this passage.

Principle One: Contentment is not automatic but must be learned over time.

Look how clearly Paul states this truth. In verse 11 he declares, "I have learned to be content" and in verse 12 he says, "I have learned the secret of being content." The question is - Why did Paul have to learn contentment? Why wasn't it just given to him as a gift from God? God is most glorified when we struggle through the process of being weaned from our dependence on the things of the world. The picture is one only a mother can fully understand. A child is born and for a long time he looks to his mother's breast as the source of his nourishment. Breakfast, lunch and supper all come from the same place. When he is hungry, he cries and his mother knows exactly what to do. Her milk satisfies him and back to sleep he goes. But the day comes when he has to learn how to take a bottle. He cries, big tears roll down his face, his arms reach out but his mother pushes them away. He fights, he pouts, he screams, all to no avail. What has happened to mum? She who used to be his friend has now become his enemy. If mum has a heart at all, she cries too because from now on things will be different. When the battle is over, when the tears have stopped, when he learns to eat with his brothers and sisters, then the child comes, lays his head on his mother's breast, not in order to be fed, but just because he wants to be near her.

Here is the truth: Unless a mother weans her child, he will never grow up. Though it may seem hard, and though the child misunderstands, if a mother truly loves her child, she will not stop until her child has been weaned from her breast. When the job is done, the child no longer begs for that which once seemed indispensable. Once he could not live without his mother's milk; now he no longer needs it.

To be weaned is to have something removed from your life which you thought you couldn't live without. Most of us live on the opposite principle. In our hearts we think, "I would be happy if only I had a new car or a new job or a new dress or a new husband or a new wife." Since life is hardly ever that simple, we stay frustrated when we ought to be happy. No wonder we are never satisfied. Instead of being weaned from the world, we are wedded to it. Or maybe I should say, welded to it.

Principle Two: Happiness depends on circumstances; Contentment comes from my confidence in God.

Verse 12 lays this out very clearly. "I know what it is to be in need, and I know what it is to have plenty." In case we missed it he adds this phrase, "Whether well fed or hungry, whether living in plenty or in want". It's easy to assume Paul means being well fed is good and going hungry is bad. But that's not correct. Poverty and prosperity both have their good uses - and both can lead us astray spiritually. If we take the words of Jesus seriously, riches can wreck the soul much quicker than poverty.

The comedy film *Cool Running* is about the first Jamaican bobsled team to go to the Winter Olympics. John Candy plays a former American gold medallist who becomes a coach for the Jamaican team. The players grow to like the American coach and affectionately dub him "Sled-god." Late in the story the coach's dark history comes out. In an Olympics following his gold medal performance, he broke the rules by weighting the U.S. sled, bringing disgrace on himself and his team. One of the Jamaican bobsledders could not understand why anyone who had already won a gold medal would cheat. Finally he nervously asked Candy to explain.
"I thought I had to win," said the coach. *"But I learned something. If you are not happy without a gold medal, you won't be happy with it, either."*

Paul knew that riches are not the way to contentment. So he was willing to hold material things with an open hand. He refused to become a slave to wealth. He could walk away from prosperity when service to the Lord demanded it. What about you? Are you killing yourself to get that gold medal? Let me remind you – if you're not happy without it, you won't be happy with it either.

Note the principles, they are important.

Contentment is not automatic but must be learned over time.

Happiness depends on circumstances; Contentment comes from my confidence in God.

Principle Three: Contentment rests on great truths.

God has ordained every circumstance of my life. I know of no truth more important than this. If you were asked this week why the wicked prosper while the righteous often suffer in this world, what would you say? I constantly face this question in dealing with the seeming inequities of life. Hardly a week goes by that I don't get a letter, phone call or email to our radio studios from someone in a tough time, often battling with cancer. What I can't explain is why it happens to one person and not to another.

Some years ago I was given a test in a hospital to see if I had a cancer behind one of my eyes. That's a little scary no matter how healthy you feel. The results were good - no evidence of cancer. But as I thought about it, it occurred to me that from a human point of view I had simply dodged a bullet. And maybe only temporarily. You can go through life asking, "Why did this happen?" And you'll end up frustrated and disappointed because in this life there is rarely a satisfactory answer to that question. We simply don't know why some people live long and prosper while others never seem to catch a break. In the world's terms, they are victims of bad luck. From the standpoint of Holy Scripture, we can only say that God is working out His plan in ways we can't see from our limited vantage point. This becomes very personal when I pray with members of our radio audience as they face the uncertainties of life. One thing I've learned is that there are no guarantees, which is why a long time ago I stopped making promises about what God will do in a particular situation. Generally, I don't know what God is going to do, and I'm content to leave matters in His hands.

In verse 12 Paul says "I have learned the secret of being content." Don't you love secrets? It's always fun when anyone says, "Let me tell you a secret." So what is the secret of contentment? I think the answer can be found in two phrases.

First, in verse 11 he mentions "whatever the circumstances," and then in verse 12 he says "in any and every situation". Those two phrases would appear to cover all that life has to offer. The secret of contentment lies in understanding that nothing happens by chance, but everything is *ordained* by the hand of a loving God. I like the word "ordained" because it is a very strong word. I know that some people may think it smacks of *fatalism* but to me it simply means that God is in charge of all the details of life - the good and the bad, the positive, the negative - and He has ordained not only what happens to us, but when it happens, how it happens, where it happens, what happens before it happens, and what happens after it happens.

I know it's easy to get hung up on that, and to worry about things like *predestination* - which is a very biblical concept. It helps to remember that from our point of view we simply see events unfold topsy-turvy, almost like a handful of dice that come rolling out of the sky. Everything seems random, nothing seems to have a purpose. And so we react to life as it comes, not knowing what tomorrow will bring. Here's where biblical faith comes in. As I stand and watch those dice rolling all around me, I can look up and see the invisible hand of God blowing on the dice so that the numbers come up just the way He wants. Nothing happens by chance. There is no such thing as luck or fate or kismet or *happenstance.* Contentment is possible when I realise that everything happens for a purpose - whether I see it or not. Usually I don't see it as it unfolds before me - and often I never fully understand it even in retrospect. This is where the *First Rule of the Spiritual Life* becomes so helpful: *He's God and we're not.*

That leads me to a personal question. Are you willing to let God be God in your life? Or do you intend to tell Him how to do His job? You can be God or He can be God—and there's nothing in between those two options. As long as you try to be God, you'll be miserable, frustrated, and very discontented because you were not made to run the universe - not even the little patch of it you call your life. Even that small patch belongs to God - and you'll never be happy or content until you surrender your right to run your own life and let God be God in all things.

So, Contentment rests on two great truths:
1) *That God has ordained every circumstance of my life.*
2) *That God will give me strength in every circumstance to do his will.*

This is the true meaning of Philippians 4:13, "I can do all things through Christ who gives me strength." This verse, wonderful as it is, has sometimes been misused by well-meaning believers who make it say more than Paul intended. Occasionally people say things like "You can do whatever you want to do – see Philippians 4:13", as if it were a magic formula that could make me a millionaire or give me wings to fly through the air. The phrase "all things" must be defined by its context. Paul is talking about being content in every circumstance - whether he had plenty or whether he had next to nothing. Verse 13 explains how he managed to live above his circumstances. He did it only by the power of Jesus Christ dwelling in him. For him, the secret of contentment was not a stiff upper lip or a positive mental attitude. He was content precisely because he had learned to rely completely on Jesus Christ.

This takes more than positive thinking. You've got to have Jesus Christ on the inside. Are we who believe better than other people? No. Do we suffer? Yes. What makes the difference? We have the power of the indwelling Christ who gives us the strength we need.

Is it enough? Is Jesus Christ enough for the problems of life? Is His broken body enough? Is His shed blood sufficient? Is His intercession in heaven able to sustain us? Can His power meet the problems of life? Yes, yes, a thousand times yes, and the believers across the ages testify that Jesus Christ is enough. Show me a truly contented person and I'll show you a miracle. In this fallen world contentment cannot be explained apart from the supernatural power of Jesus Christ. The beauty is that if you're not a content person, if you haven't experienced that miracle, you can – simply by learning to lean on the Lord.

Basis for a contented life

Let me ask you this: What will you do with what you have read? What does your future hold in store for the world, your family and for you personally? No one but God can answer those questions. But there is one thing we know. God has given us everything we need for today. Therefore we can be content whatever happens, and we need not fear the future.

To become a *contented person...* it can't get much better than that. A friend wrote and mentioned how people are worried with the high terrorist alert. And in his city, crime is up. It's another variation on the theme, what does the future hold? Looking at it from "under the sun", nobody knows anything, the main thing is to stay alive, it's all in God's hands, and you can't even be sure of Him. Put God back in the picture, though, and the whole scene brightens. The righteous one says, with full trust, "My future is in your hands."

We know that the future is *certain*.
We worry about how and when we will die, about jobs and marriages, or the lack of them. These are mere details. We know what is important to know, that is, no future threat can overcome the saving power of Christ, and no future force can separate us from the love of God. If I am guaranteed His power on the one hand and His love on the other, I am set for life - and beyond. So, the future is *certain.*

We know the future is *ours*.

Paul wrote to Corinthian Christians who were dividing up a spiritual pie, when all of them could have all of it. "For all things are yours... the world or life or death or the present or THE FUTURE - all are yours, and you are Christ's, and Christ is God's"

Let's get a handle on what it means for the future to be ours. Paul's terms of the world, life, death, things present or things to come "are all the great powers that govern the life of man and before which he feels his smallness and dependence."

Gordon Fee called them the "tyrannies of existence," but for the Christian they become "gifts of God to assist and to enrich them, they constitute positive forces for good..."

We know the future is *close*.

Dare we ask - What does the near future hold?

Some look to the future with dread and fear. The Christian, however, sees it as providing opportunity to serve the Lord, preach the Good News, and bring him one step closer to eternity's gate. This is because he belongs to Christ, and Christ to God, who holds the future in his hands. Meanwhile I hope you will settle back and do what you have God's strength for this one day. Turn off your *transporter* to tomorrow. Learn to live by one of Oswald Chambers' favourite sayings. He would say, "I refuse to worry." And if you find yourself worrying about the future, would you ask God to beam you back up to where it's safe - in your *today*.

Chapter 8
The 'Feel Good' Factor

Life is somewhat about continual learning. I think I am more aware of learning now than when I was younger. Someone shared an email with me titled "Interesting things you learn when you have sons":

A king size waterbed holds enough water to fill a 2000 square foot house 4 inches deep with water.
A three year old boy's voice is louder than 200 adults in a crowded restaurant.
If you hook a dog leash over a ceiling fan, the motor is not strong enough to let a 42 pound boy fly around the room, even if he is wearing Batman underwear and a superman cape.

We are in one of the most unusual times in history ever yet experienced. We are turned on and tuned into 24/7 news and information. We want to know 'why?' and 'how?' and 'when?' about everything. We want to know actions and reactions as well as the statistics that result from those things. We can go at any time to our television or computers and find out almost anything about anything, yet even then we sometime refuse to act on the knowledge we access. But it all seems to make us even more a worried generation.

To be sure there's some worry that's good for us. Worry can alert us to danger threatening our health and safety. But often enough worry can capsize our boat. Fretting and anxiety can rock it. The forecast for all of us as life goes by is of course that there will be challenges, heartaches, disappointments, and maybe some trauma or fear-inducing events. However, if we stabilise the worry in our lives, the next few months can be great months. Friends and family will get sick. Finances may test us. Relationships will have tense moments. Our immediate family may experience transition. Through all these we have the choice to worry or to trust God amidst it all. We all worry, but excessive worry can be a choice. We, therefore, must take action ahead of time so that worry will not wear us down. We can adopt a life-long plan that will take the sting out of worry, take an axe to anxiety, and whip the wind out of the fear which fuels worry.

Wouldn't we all want a worry-free life? If so, we need to learn to respond to challenges and disappointments in ways that will strengthen us. So I am going to write about worry and depression (a more severe form of worry), and how we can feel good for most of the time. Much of my thinking on worry comes from decades of observing and counselling people. But I've noticed that King David had a good perspective on this. I will be referring to his words in 2 Samuel 22 – I think it has a lot to say to us.

Now, remember some worry is good. It keeps some high risk-takers away from the cliffs. But there is a kind of worry that can lay siege on us night and day. This toxic worry can catapult fear and anxiety on us until the defensive walls of our hearts eventually break down. This unrelenting worry has been called, "toxic worry". The more vulnerable we *feel* (regardless of how vulnerable we actually are) and the less control we *feel* we have (regardless of how much control we actually have), the more toxic our worrying will become. Therefore, any steps we can take to reduce our *feelings* of vulnerability and/or increase our *feelings* of control will serve to reduce our feelings of toxic worry."

Feelings

Most of our feelings do not originate from events but rather from the self-talk we give ourselves in response to events. In fact, our self-talk is a major determining factor of our happiness and joy. If it is negative self-talk, we tell ourselves, *"There is no chance. All is lost. I am doomed. Woe is me. Everyone is against me."* When we say such things to ourselves, we are well on our way to toxic worry and a life that is negative, unhappy and pessimistic. We must watch our self-talk because it can cause us to be in a state of chronic negativity over circumstances that start out fairly innocuous.

It's been said that *worry* is a special form of fear. To create worry we elongate fear with anticipation and memory, expand it in imagination, and fuel it with emotion. But not all worry is the same. Some worries are signs of conditions, like post-traumatic disorders, anxiety disorders or depression. Some come from shyness as part of a genetic temperament. Some just come from everyday life. However, much of worry in life is self inflicted, and it comes unnecessarily. We must not let fear and worry rule our lives. Fear kills ministry. Worry breeds lack of confidence. Worry weakens self-esteem. It kills the courage in us to risk it all for God. Fear makes us play it safe. Worry makes us timid. Worry wears us down. Have you ever had a worry consume you? You think about it all the time. Fear overcomes you. You worry you are not good enough. You worry that you will not be liked. You worry you won't be taken care of.

Steps to controlling worry

A survey of primary care physicians reported that "at least one third of office visits were prompted by some form of anxiety." This is probably not much of a surprise to us. Here is a four-step plan to stop or alleviate the worry in our lives. So take note or suffer by worrying for the rest of your lives!

Step One: Keep as physically well as you can.

That doesn't sound too spiritual! But in 1 Corinthians, the apostle Paul says that our body is the temple of God. Our body is where the Holy Spirit resides. Our body was created by God. We have His image in us. God wants us to keep our "temples" in shape. Whether young or old, we need to know that some form of exercise is one of the best, natural anti-anxiety, anti-worry agents we have. You may think, "I am too old to exercise." No, no one is too old for exercise. Most of us can walk. Or we can do some slow movements to flex ourselves.

Exercise is good for the brain. It releases a natural antidepressant. It reduces tension. It drains off excessive aggression. It lowers frustration. It keeps us feeling limber. It heightens our alertness. It gives us a sense of well being, It makes us feel good. It improves sleep. It makes us feel rested. It stops us from casual overeating. It helps us focus. It lowers blood pressure. It lowers cholesterol. It can start with just walking. We may say that we don't exercise because we are too busy. And when we get too busy, we get tired. When we get tired, we feel vulnerable and have a lack of control. When we feel vulnerable and out of control, the formula says, we worry! I am the first to admit that I need to exercise more. But we all need to.

Step Two: Get the true facts about what is concerning us.

In the old TV show called "Dragnet" they would say, "The facts, ma'am, just the facts." Worry is often not based on fact. It is based on fear. It is based on assumptions. And assumptions are defined as the lowest form of information. When we don't have the facts, our imagination comes in and creates such a commotion of fear that imagination becomes worse than reality. We envision the worst possible predicament. We must watch our self-talk because it can cause us to be in a state of chronic negativity... but facts can short-circuit the fear.

Here's an example of how imagination increases worry and how facts can stop it. We say, "I made a mistake last week and now everyone in the company laughs at me." "Really? Everyone in the company is laughing at you?" "Well, no, not everyone in the company, but everyone in my department is." "Really? Everyone in the department?" "Well, maybe not each and everyone. But, boy, you should have seen them smirking." "Really? How many people do you really think are laughing at you? Did anyone say anything negative to you in the last week?" "No. Well, maybe John." "Okay, John. Anyone else?" "No, just John." So we went from everyone in the company, to everyone in the department, to many are smirking, to really just John. One person! The fact is John, who is one person, is critical of you, and maybe it is his problem and not yours.

On one hand, facts can intensify the worrying, but in the long run we are much better off with the facts than without them. Whenever we are in a tailspin, we must look at the facts and not just our feelings or worry will get out of hand.

Let's go to a more serious topic than one person laughing at us. Worries are really rumours that we start about ourselves. We start a rumour like, "Well, maybe I am in trouble." And suddenly we believe our own rumour and say, "I'm in trouble? Yikes! I'm in trouble!" Worry is often based on the myth of a rumour *that we started*. How's that for mental illness? Opinions, possibilities, even probabilities made me worry, but facts stopped the worry.

Let me go one step further. I know there are people reading who are suffering from disease. I would say we still need to have a handle on our worry and know the stages of worry and even grief and move on through that. Psalm 23 says, "Though I walk through the valley of death..." The fact that King David wrote the Psalm and used the phrase "though I walk *through* the valley of death," meant we are *never* to stop in the valley of our worry, depression, grief or death itself. We are to always walk *through* the valley and get out of it. We are not to stop and stay in it. When people lose a loved one or come up against a challenge, some stop in the "valley of death". They never get out of it. They never move on. They never lift the blinds of their windows, instead they just sit in the darkness of despair. The fact of the promise of God's grace and heaven for those who trust Him is a fact we must never forget. Facts always help. Which brings me to another step on how to combat worry.

Step Three: Stay connected.

Never worry alone. The Bible uses these words in Galatians 6:2, "Bear ye one another's burdens, and so fulfil the law of Christ." Amazing! Did you ever read it in that context? If you do not bear one another's burdens, we do not fulfil Christ's design, His laws of living here on this earth. His basic principle of living is to bear one another's burdens!

When we start worrying, the tendency is just to talk to ourselves and list our woes and our inadequacies, which then creates a perceived heightened vulnerability and fear of lack of control. And that equals toxic worry. When we are worried we really need someone to talk to - a friend, a pastor, a Christian brother or sister. Someone who can relay the facts to us and not the rumours; someone who can show us when we are getting illogical in our anxiety. Those who fret, worry or panic on their own are on a slippery slope. I am always saddened by the discovery of relationships that are on the brink. I wish the couple had come to the church earlier for help. When we worry with someone and when we stay connected, we find out that our self-perceptions are often wrong. We find out that our despair is misplaced and that there is actually more hope than we think.

Sometimes, people don't reach out because they think no one can help, or no one knows the problem well enough to offer any suggestions that he hasn't already thought of. But the point of reaching out is not just to get solutions. Even more important, it is to get a feeling, the feeling of support. Parents, do all you can to make your child have a connected childhood. If not with you, then with the church or an uncle or aunt so that when trouble comes later you may be able to intervene. It might just be simple guidance and support because there is a connection there already.

Let me sum up what we've seen so far in this chapter -
1) Keep as physically well as you can.
2) Get the true facts about what is concerning us.
3) Stay connected.
Which brings us to the next step.

Step Four: God can help us.

We need not worry for we can have a personal relationship with God who *wants* to help us. When we say, "There is nothing we can't solve as a team," we need to know that God wants to be part of our team!

I think this song of King David was written towards the end of his life (2 Samuel 22). Possibly the very last song David wrote. He is overwhelmed by all the battles, deaths, betrayal, famine and suffering he has experienced in his long career as the musician shepherd boy turned warrior king. But the psalm he wrote is not a dark dirge. No, it is his song of faith telling us that we need not ever worry because no matter how high a wall is, no matter how wide the river is, no matter how many troops are marching against you, there *ain't* no mountain high enough to stop God's love; no mountain high enough to make David forget the words of his supreme song.

2 Samuel 22:1, "David sang to the Lord the words of this song when the Lord delivered him from the hand of all his enemies and from the hand of Saul. He said: "The Lord is my rock, my fortress and my deliverer; my God is my rock, in whom I take refuge, my shield and the horn of my salvation. He is my stronghold, my refuge and my saviour - from violent men you save me. I call to the Lord, who is worthy of praise, and I am saved from my enemies. The waves of death swirled about me; the torrents of destruction overwhelmed me. The cords of the grave coiled around me; the snares of death confronted me. In my distress I called to the Lord; I called out to my God. From his temple he heard my voice; my cry came to his ears."

The bottom line is that we can know for a fact that God exists, that He is loving and that He hears us when we call out to Him in distress. He is a personal God who cares for each individual, created uniquely and lovingly in our mother's womb. This God knows we have troubles, but He sent His Son, Jesus, to live for us so we ultimately need not worry.

Jesus taught us that: "Can any of you by worrying add a single hour to your span of life? So do not worry about tomorrow, for tomorrow will bring worries of its own". Today's trouble is enough for today. This same Jesus fought for us, prayed for us, got beaten for us, and was executed to save us so we need not worry needlessly. He wanted us to know that if we accept Him into our lives and follow Him we could then focus on Him and the possibilities that He could bring, whether from darkness to light, from despair to hope and from death to life. Therefore, what do we need to fear? This Jesus can perform miracles. He brought a little girl and a man named Lazarus back to life, demon possessed and abused women to hope and unethical, broken-down men to new life. His heavenly Father offers that to us today.

David intimately knew this God. It was because of this God that we can look at David's life and see that David feared no giant named Goliath, or a boss named Saul, or slanderers like Shimei, or thousands of Philistine soldiers, or Saul who plotted to kill him, or his son, Absalom, who betrayed him. No, in spite of all of that, he wrote this song that he need not ever worry in life for the Almighty God was indeed his rock, his fortress and his shield.

If we can grab hold of that then we, some thousands of years later, need not have the self-talk that there is no hope. We need not fear the unknown. Why? Because we know one thing. The Lord is our rock. From God's rock we can find a place high enough to use as a look-out place and see the facts as they truly are. From God's rock we find a fortress to harbour us from the storms of life. From God's rock we find a shield to protect us. From God's rock we can find a stand to blow the horn of salvation. For God is our stronghold and our refuge and for that we can forever be centred and need not worry.

Let's think a bit more about *feelings* because whether we feel good or bad is strongly determined by how we think and what we say to ourselves. All of our moods are created by our thoughts. We feel the way we do right now because of the thoughts we have at this moment. When we are feeling depressed, our thoughts go negative. That's pretty obvious. We perceive not only ourselves but also the entire world in dark, gloomy terms. Even worse is when we use this as a basis for reality, and then come to believe that things are really as bad as we imagine them. The negative thoughts that cause emotional turmoil nearly always contain gross distortions - untruths. Although negative thoughts seem valid, more often than not they are in reality irrational or just plain wrong. These untruths establish themselves as a major cause of emotional suffering. Any resulting depression, therefore, stems not from accurate perceptions of reality but from mental slippage.

Let me comment on the positive thoughts that help us feel good about ourselves. These *can't* be based purely on achievement, riches or good looks for we have seen beautiful, handsome, rich and successful people grow so unhappy that their despair drives them to end their lives. Feeling good and having healthy emotions have to be based on truth within and not just appearances and happy talk around us.

So knowing this as a framework - here come my practical points on combating the worry in our lives. Let's try and bring all that I've written thus far together and thrust it home.

We have a CHOICE.

When we face a worry, we need to know right at that point that we have a CHOICE, which is an acronym for *"Christ Has Options, I Can Ease."*

How we feel to a great extent frames how we choose to think about our circumstances and ourselves. Knowing we have choices means we don't have to be victims. Knowing we have choices means we have a way out. Knowing we have choices gives us the option to look at circumstances either negatively or positively. We can choose to look at our circumstances with a greater sense of reality instead of an imagined reality framed by suffering, negative thoughts. We can choose to throw in the towel when the going gets rough or to keep pressing on. We can choose to break or keep promises. We can choose to be generous and forgiving or stingy and unforgiving.

We choose what voices we listen to.

Why is it that some can face cancer, experience pain and yet remain upbeat in the midst of the challenge, while others faced with the same dire situation become depressed? For the most part, people have a choice of how they think about the obstacles in their lives. Often a given situation in and of itself is not the source of worry or depression. It is our choice to dwell on negative thoughts that produces worry and anxiety. In every situation, we have a choice, a true, honest-to-God choice to be hopeful and optimistic, or despairing and pessimistic. But to be able to make healthy emotional choices we need to use mental filters that block out bad, unrealistic thinking and gather healthy realistic thinking. The more we see the greater, bigger reality that holds good, alternative options, the more mentally and spiritually healthy we can be. The trap in negativity is that we can buy into unreal, unfair thinking about ourselves.

A Paediatrics report said that about 40 percent of 9 and 10 year old girls were trying to lose weight. It's not that 40% are overweight; it's just that most of them think they are. So who was telling them they are? Negative voices don't only come from parents. They can come from peers in our community and virtual peers, like movies, books, TV shows that overtly or subtly say that unless we look as thin or fit as the celebrities then we will not have a fulfilled life.

We have a choice to either buy into an unrealistic culture that judges us by looks, money or achievement or we can make the choice not to listen. When we worry, or get depressed, we need to be aware that our thoughts have drifted into negativity. *Self-talk* is either a killer or a blessing. But I am not here to give a pop psychology course. This was just the framework, the context. I am here to point us towards Jesus Christ. Why? Because having Jesus as the centre of our lives, having Him as our best friend, having Him as the true Lord of our lives where we follow Him and turn over every area of our lives to Him is the best thing that can ever happen to us. Whether you're a seeker who hasn't decided what you think about Jesus or a veteran believer, choosing to follow Jesus is the best decision you'll ever make. Following Him is the best antidote to toxic worry. It is reality and it is healthy, healthy, healthy. Why? Because with Christ we never can be a loser and we need not worry. Jesus looked at the so-called "losers of the world" and said,

"Hey, I love you and we can change the way the world works. You are of great value to Me, so much so that I gave my life for you. If you look at Jesus' sermons, His big message was, "Trust God; don't worry; live by the Spirit and grace, and not by the Law." The Apostle Paul jumps in and says, "Do not worry about anything, but in everything by prayer and supplication with thanksgiving let your requests be made known to God."

A positive attitude is one of the great worry-deflators.

Knowing this we should discard the negative thoughts about ourselves. We can live with our heads held high, expectant of God's blessings and will upon us. The life He calls us to is not easy nor rewarded with worldly riches, success or good looks, but it is a life that has meaning even in the midst of suffering. It is a life that holds hope, provides options, gives fulfilment and joy even in the midst of worry and difficulties.

But let's go even further back once again to when King David was around, in the Old Testament. Here was a man who had armies after him. Notice how it shows that all things are fair and reasonable because God has integrity, is faithful, pure and just. And when we have God at the centre of our lives, all that toxic worry stuff can stop because we have a true reference in life. God gives us an accurate picture of who we are and how valuable we are. Remember, the sign of the cross is a positive, not a negative. And for that, we should always choose to follow God, be optimistic and not worry. Amen?

Chapter 9
When 'Things' Don't Work Out

What do we do when *'things'* don't work out. That can be a big cause for worry eating away at us. Do you have any failed dreams? Things not come together in the way that you would like? So – we look back with regret and forward with uncertainty.

Roald Amundsen was a Norwegian explorer who dreamed of becoming the first person in recorded history to reach the North Pole. In 1908 Amundsen received government and private funding, gathered supplies and recruited a crew. Then he received news that an American had reached the North Pole and his dream was shattered. Amundsen did not cancel his planned expedition but secretly planned a different destination. He didn't even tell his ship's crew until after they left Norway that they were headed not to the Arctic but to Antarctica. Amundsen was going to the South Pole. Antarctica is among the most dangerous and extreme climates and terrain on earth. Their ship reached the seventh continent in 1911. Amundsen carefully prepared, setting out across the ice with four men, 42 dogs and four sledges in October 1911. It turned out to be a race. The English explorer Robert Scott was heading for the South Pole from a different direction. The winner would go down in history as one of the greatest explorers and pioneers of all time. In December 1911 Amundsen's party was closing in on the exact location. His men told him to go first. Roald Amundsen reached the spot and planted the Norwegian flag in the name of their king. At that historic moment Amundsen's men told him to make a speech. Roald Amundsen then said, "I wanted to go to the North Pole".

He had a dream but his dream was unfulfilled. Even though he accomplished one of the greatest feats of human endeavour all he could think about was the dream that didn't come true. Few of us have ever yearned to reach the North Pole, but we are all dreamers. We imagined the way we wanted life to be. We pictured ourselves as successful, healthy and happy. We wanted to be married, rich, thin, tall, pretty, famous or powerful. We wanted a house, a baby, a business or a cottage in France. We expected our children to pick up where we left off and be better than we ever became. We thought we could write the script of life and live happily ever after.

We have all dreamed and then some of the dreams didn't come true. The marriage didn't happen. The child wasn't born. The team didn't win. The happiness didn't come. The pain never went away. We feel cheated. Perhaps we are deeply disappointed. Maybe even angry and bitter. It is as if we are living somebody else's life, trapped in a biography that is more of a nightmare than a dream. At first we think that our unfulfilled dream is merely a temporary setback on the way to something even better. But then it doesn't get better. It gets worse. We begin to wonder if there is any point in dreaming again. We wonder if there is any point in anticipating tomorrow when we didn't even deal with yesterday's failed plans.

We are not talking about the kind of dreams that show on the screens of our minds when sleeping at night. Sleep dreams have been thoroughly researched. They typically rehearse and rewrite what we did and thought about during the day before we fell asleep. To be sure, they are psychologically and physically important. Sleep dreams are primarily about the past. We are talking about wide-awake dreams. These are the dreams of hope and a future. They look at life and imagine the way we want it to be. We observe all the possible options and choose the ones we like best.

Dreams are important. Dreams give us hope. Dreams show us the way. Dreams help us to anticipate the way we want things to become. It is our way of visualizing ourselves in a preferred tomorrow. If we could not dream we would be trapped in yesterday and today. There would be no faith, for faith is always about the future.

The Bible is a catalogue of dreamers. God dreamed of a Garden of Eden. Eve and Adam dreamed of eating fruit that would make them better than God. Noah dreamed of an ark. Moses dreamed of his people set free from slavery. Hannah dreamed of becoming pregnant. David dreamed of a temple in Jerusalem. Hosea dreamed of getting his wife back from prostitution. Zebedee's wife dreamed of her sons (James and John) sitting on either side of Jesus in heaven. Jesus dreamed that someday God's will would be done on earth as it is done in heaven. But dreams don't always come true.

One of the Bible's dreamers was a Hebrew woman named Naomi. She was a good and godly person who lived in Bethlehem over 3000 years ago. Her dream was to be a wife and a mother, to live a happy domestic life at home. Then came a bad economy, unemployment and famine. Her husband Elimelech told her that they had to move - to Moab. Moab was a different country with different customs and language. It was not where she dreamed to be. Naomi bore two sons and named them Mahlon and Kilion. Her dream of motherhood came true. She loved her boys and was deeply proud of them. Then one awful day her husband died and part of her dream died with him. All her dreams focused on her sons. She dreamed that they would marry godly Jewish women and give her grandchildren that would fill the hollow place in her life. Mahlon and Kilion came home with Moabite girls and wanted to marry them. It was against all she believed. The Old Testament forbade marriage to unbelievers. But her sons married them anyway and broke Naomi's heart. Thinking she had suffered the worst and that there were no more dreams left to shatter Naomi was blasted with the double barrels of her two beloved sons dying. There are no pains like losing your children. When a husband or wife dies you are called a widow or widower. When your parents die you are called an orphan. When your child dies there is no word to describe who you are. It is the shattering of dreams too painful to have its own word. Naomi changed her name. Naomi means "my delight" but there was nothing delightful left in her life. She called herself Mara, which means "bitter." Unfulfilled dreams had turned her into a bitter woman.

What about our dreams?

When our dreams are unfulfilled we can't help but wonder why. Sometimes the answer is not hard to find - just difficult to hear.

Some dreams are unfulfilled because they never should have been dreamed at all.

We assume an entitlement to have whatever we want. If we want it we assume that God is obligated to give it. If we dream, we assume that it will automatically happen. Since childhood we have been told, "You can do anything!" This is simply not true. I do not have what it takes to be a professional athlete or an amateur musician. When unrealistic and inappropriate dreams are unfulfilled we have not been cheated or deceived, we merely dreamed the wrong dream.

Some dreams are unfulfilled because they would have been bad for us.

It is the love of God that keeps us from some of our dreams. We would have ruined our lives and the lives of others if everything happened according to our plan. God protected us from ourselves.

Some dreams are fulfilled but feel unfulfilling.

We dreamed that we would be happy if only we got what we wanted but then found that what we dreamed for didn't actually work. Our standard of living has significantly increased during the past fifty years but there has been no increase in the number of people who say they are happy. New possessions, realized ambitions and desired success didn't produce what we expected.

Naomi must have wondered why. Her dream didn't seem bold or unreasonable. She did not dream of fame or wealth or power. There is no record of her praying for a miracle. She wanted a husband. She wanted a happy marriage. She wanted godly sons to marry godly Jewish wives. She wanted her sons to outlive her. They didn't seem like big dreams but they were not fulfilled.

Tell me about your unfulfilled dream. What has left you in some form of worry because it hasn't worked out how you dreamed? Years ago what did you dream for today? Successful career. Less weight. Engagement and a wedding. Children. Health. Happiness. Reconciliation. Some destination like the North Pole. University degree. Children who loved and lived for God. Making the team. Love. Acceptance. Friends. House. Job or position - Tell me about your unfulfilled dream.

Job was a wealthy successful man who lost his children, fortune, friends and health. His life was a nightmare. Read what he said. "My days have passed, my plans are shattered, and so are the desires of my heart" (Job 17:11). When our dreams are gone we turn to God. Isaiah 40:28-31 states it so well, "Do you not know? Have you not heard? The Lord is the everlasting God, the Creator of the ends of the earth. He will not grow tired or weary, and his understanding no one can fathom. He gives strength to the weary and increases the power of the weak. Even youths grow tired and weary, and young men stumble and fall; but those who hope in the Lord will renew their strength. They will soar on wings like eagles; they will run and not grow weary, they will walk and not be faint." God gives grace to those with broken dreams. He does not guarantee that our dreams will come true but that He will give us strength to go on.

Why would God not fulfil our dreams?

That is the big question. If we are His children and He loves us, why does He not give us what we want? There is an answer to this question that we may not want to hear but need to hear. God wants us centred on Him. The greatest good is the God-centred life. When all our dreams come true we do not need God. The centre of our lives is us and what we want. This is not good enough. Totally fulfilled dreams lead to self-sufficiency and self-sufficiency excludes God. The truth is that we need God more than we need our dreams fulfilled. So, will we of shattered dreams ever dream again? There is a curious line that appears several times in the Bible. Let's read Joel 2:28. God says... "I will pour out my Spirit on all people. Your sons and daughters will prophesy, your old men will dream dreams, your young men will see visions." While these words are primarily a prophecy about the future they contain a principle from God: *God causes even old men to dream new dreams.* When circumstances or age indicate that our dreaming days are over God helps us to dream again. God designed us to be dreamers. He gives us new dreams when old dreams don't happen.

Have you ever seen the adverts for Kit-Cars? They can be a place for dreaming. I can imagine myself driving a car that turns heads. They look great! But in those same magazines are adverts for *"parts cars."* Some cars are dreams-come-true. Some cars might become dreams-come-true if you spend a lot of money and time fixing them up. But then there are the *"parts cars"*. "*Parts cars*" were once somebody's dream but now are good only to supply the parts to build other cars. Our unfulfilled dreams can be the "*parts cars*" in the driveway of God. He can and will use pieces of our broken dreams to turn our new dreams into classics.

That's what happened to Naomi. She did not get her husband or her sons back to life again. Her former dreams were forever gone. But, God took the left over pieces of her old dream to give a new dream and make it come true. One of her daughters-in-law was named Ruth. She loved Naomi and believed in Naomi's God. When Naomi returned to her hometown of Bethlehem, Ruth came with her. She remarried and gave birth to a son named Obed. The baby Obed was laid in the lap of the woman who changed her name back again. Mara of bitterness again became Naomi of delight. The women of Bethlehem were thrilled to see Naomi dream again. She dreamed of a godly grandson. She dreamed of a family tree that would make a difference. She looked at the baby she loved and dreamed of tomorrow. Her grandson Obed grew up and had a grandson of his own, named David. David became the king of Israel and bore a family line that included a man called "The Son of David." His name was Jesus. God took the leftover parts of Naomi's broken dream and made them into Jesus Christ, the Saviour of the world.

Listen, you of unfulfilled dreams! And worrying about it all - Do not become bitter because life has not turned out the way you planned. Turn your heart and hope to Jesus. He will give you strength to get you beyond yesterday's disappointment. Trust him and don't be afraid to dream again. Trust him to make new dreams come true out of the pieces of the old dreams that were shattered. Consider Psalm 37 verses 4 to 7: "Delight yourself in the Lord and he will give you the desires of your heart. Commit your way to the Lord; trust in him and he will do this: He will make your righteousness shine like the dawn, the justice of your cause like the noonday sun. Be still before the Lord and wait patiently for him."

The following quote comes from an email: *"One night, while my young son was sleeping, a storm began brewing outside. After a loud clap of thunder I heard him wake up, so I headed toward his room to comfort him. He asked me to stay with him until he fell asleep. As I lay there I realised he hadn't asked me to make the storm go away, but to stay with him. How many times, I wondered, have I asked God to take away the storms of life, when instead I need to ask him to stay with me and help me weather them more peacefully?"*

What a beautiful thought! Paul put it richly when he wrote: "Blessed be the God and Father of our Lord Jesus Christ, the Father of mercies and God of all comfort, who comforts us in all our tribulation, that we may be able to comfort those who are in any trouble, with the comfort with which we ourselves are comforted by God."

Years ago I came across this passage in Zephaniah 3:17, "The LORD your God is with you, he is mighty to save. He will take great delight in you, he will quiet you with his love, he will rejoice over you with singing." I thought of my life. I thought of what the passage says about God and how He feels about me. He is mighty to save. He will take great delight in me. He will quiet me with His love. He will rejoice over me. I confessed that although I do not know if I fully understand what it means to be quieted by His love, I do know that there is something inside me that says, I need that. As I pondered more I prayed, Lord, please quiet me with Your love. Lord, please quiet me with Your love. Lord, please quiet me with Your love. Lord, I get loud sometimes. Not so much verbally loud, but my spirit gets loud. My heart gets loud. My mind gets loud. The world around me gets loud and the loudness overwhelms me to the point that everything within me and around me seems to be loud. So, Lord, please quiet me with Your love. In these times of unrest and confusion in our nation and world I need to be quieted by Your love. Decisions are being made that may well change the way we live and function as a people. Lord, please quiet me with Your love. As the years pass more rapidly than my mind can comprehend, I need to be quieted with Your love. I cannot keep up. I try, but I seem to fall farther and farther behind. Lord, please quiet me with Your love. In times of discouragement when I have failed to live like You have asked me to live I need to be quieted by Your love. In times of disappointment over dreams that have faded and when other people have failed to live up to my expectations, I need to be quieted by Your love. Lord, please quiet me with Your love. In times of loss and when my heart has been broken, I need to be quieted by Your love. In times of sadness when a joyful spirit seems too much to consider, I need to be quieted by Your love. Lord, please quiet me with Your love. In times of suffering and pain as the result of another's actions or my own, I need to be quieted by Your love. In times of distress and anxiety over all that I must do, or feel that I must do, I need to be quieted by Your love. In times when life is so loud that I cannot hear my own thoughts, I need to be quieted by Your love. Lord, please quiet me with Your love. Unless You quiet me with Your love my life will surely be filled with noises that may drown Your voice from my ears.

Lord, I need to be quieted by Your love. When I remind myself that You are with me, when I contemplate Your power, when I consider that You take great delight in me and when I think of You rejoicing over me with singing because of Your love for me, I am quieted. My heart is quieted. My spirit rests. "The LORD your God is with you, he is mighty to save. He will take great delight in you, he will quiet you with his love, he will rejoice over you with singing."

Chapter 10
Worry-Busters!

Lots of churches have a printed bulletin, and when there are printed words, there are bound to be some misprints - and the results are often hilarious. Here are my favourite church bloopers, actual excerpts from church bulletins:

The music ministry invites any member of the congregation who enjoys sinning to join the choir.

Ladies, please support the rummage sale. Here's a chance to get rid of those old things not worth keeping around the house. Don't forget to bring your husbands.

Missionary Bertha Belch will speak at Calvary Church tonight. Come hear Bertha Belch all the way from Africa.

And last: *Don't let worry kill you – let our pastor help.*

I brought this list to your attention because the last blooper leads into the contents of this chapter. Worry *can* kill you - and we want to help. We don't want to help kill you; we want to help you learn how to deal with worry.

Bobby McFerrin wrote and recorded a song entitled *"Don't Worry – Be Happy."* It was one of those songs that you either loved or hated. A lot of people must have loved it because it went to number one in the charts for a while. One of the lines said:

"In every life we have some trouble,
when you worry, you make it double,
don't worry – be happy."

The phrase, *"don't worry – be happy"* was repeated over and over in the song. Bobby was half right. He got the "don't worry" part correct, but when you know the Lord, you understand that faithfulness is better than happiness. Jesus' advice is better. He says, "Don't worry – *be faithful!"*

Let's focus on Luke 12:22 to 28. Jesus said to his disciples, "Do not worry about your life, what you will eat; or about your body, what you will wear. Life is more than food, and the body more than clothes. Consider the ravens: They do not sow or reap, they have no storeroom or barn; yet God feeds them. And how much more valuable you are than birds! Who of you by worrying can add a single hour to his life? Since you cannot do this very little thing, why do you worry about the rest? "Consider how the lilies grow. They do not labour or spin. Yet I tell you, not even Solomon in all his splendour was dressed like one of these. If that is how God clothes the grass of the field, which is here today, and tomorrow is thrown into the fire, how much more will he clothe you, O you of little faith! And do not set your heart on what you will eat or drink; do not worry about it. For the pagan world runs after all such things, and your Father knows that you need them. But seek his kingdom, and these things will be given to you as well."

None of us are immune from the problems of life that would tempt us to worry but as the song says, we all have trouble, but when you worry about it you have doubled your trouble. Often, you can't control the problems that come your way, but you *can* control whether or not you worry about those problems.

Let us notice three important facts about worry, and then I want to share with you five worry-busters from the Bible.

Facts about worry.

First: Worry is harmful!

We've all met people who are addicted to worry. We laugh about them and call them worry warts or *worry-holics*. But that's like laughing about someone who has cancer. Both the Bible and medical science agree that worry is harmful to your spiritual and physical health. Excessive worry, or what I call toxic worry, can make you sick, it can cut down your enjoyment of life, and it can hamper your productivity. Toxic worry is bad for every system in your body: it increases the risk of heart attacks and strokes, it impairs digestion, it causes shortness of breath, it causes all kinds of musculoskeletal aches and pains, and it produces headaches and migraines."

A newspaper columnist relates the true story of two young East Texas boys. They were given the assignment of getting rid of an old chicken snake that was causing considerable loss in the chicken coop. So they pretended they were Texas Rangers out to arrest a dangerous criminal. They put on their cowboy hats and mounted their stick horses and rode into the chicken coop to run out the old snake. They looked around the nests on the bottom shelf - no snake. Then they stood on tiptoes to uncover the nests on the top shelf. They were about to decide the snake had escaped when suddenly the old chicken snake raised its head right in front of the boys. They were so scared that both of them tried to run out of the small door of the chicken coop at the same time, in the process they did considerable damage to themselves and the chicken coop.

One of the mother's was watching from the front porch and was laughing as the boys scrambled back toward the house. She said, "Why boys, what's wrong with you? You know perfectly well that an old chicken snake can't hurt you!" Her son said, "Yes, but there's some things that'll scare you so bad that you hurt yourself!" That's exactly what worry does; it's a form of mental self-mutilation. It's harmful!

Second: Worry is useless!

Worry is a waste of time. In verse 25 Jesus asks, "Who of you by worrying can add one hour to his life?" The word He uses can also mean adding one inch to your height. Worry won't make you live longer; it will actually shorten your life. Worry won't make you any taller, instead it will cause you to be stooped over and defeated.

Our word *"worry"* comes from an Old Anglo Saxon word meaning "to strangle." When you worry, you are choking your mind and cutting off the fresh air of faith. Here's the progression. If you're a worry-holic, you think about the very worst that *might* happen, and then you imagine that it *could* happen, and then you become obsessed with fear that it *may* happen. That is the point at which healthy concern becomes unhealthy worry.

I know some wonderful people but they are *worry-holics*. It has robbed them of so much joy in life. They can even laugh about worrying so much. Their favourite line is, "Don't tell me worrying doesn't work. The things I worry the most about never happen!"

The challenges in life can be divided into two broad categories: those things you *can't* do anything about (like the weather); and those things you *can* do something about. Don't worry about the first category, because there's nothing you can do about those things. Don't worry about the second category, because if you *can* do something - do it, don't worry about it!

A little poem may help you overcome worry. It says:

> *"For every evil under the sun,*
> *Either there is a cure, or there is none.*
> *If there be one, seek 'till you find it.*
> *If there be none, never mind it!"*

Jesus said, "Do not worry" because it's a waste of time!

Third: Worry is sinful!

Worry is not just some harmless habit. I'm convinced that worry is the number 1 sin among Christians. The opposite of worry is trust in God. In verse 28 Jesus says, "Oh you of little faith!" Romans 14:23 says, "That which is not of faith is sin." When you worry, you are disobeying the Lord and demonstrating a lack of faith. God has promised He is going to take care of you. When you worry, you are actually saying, "God you are a liar! I don't really believe you are going to take care of me, so I'd better worry about this problem."

Worry is practical atheism. A *worry-holic* may not be a theological atheist, but they might as well be. You can proclaim you believe in God until your face turns blue, but when you worry you are saying, "I don't believe God exists," or "I don't believe God can be trusted to take care of me." A Christian who worries is a contradiction of terms. There is a difference between ignorance and stupidity. If you don't know any better, you may claim ignorance. But when you've been informed by God's Word and you refuse to change, that's stupidity. It's sin. As Forest Gump's mother said, "Stupid *is* as stupid *does.*" Maybe you didn't know worry was sin. Now, you know, so you can start having victory when you *confess* it as sin and *repent* of it. That means, "don't worry - be faithful."

I would be a poor teacher indeed if I told you worry was a sin but didn't give you some practical ways to stop worrying.

Biblical worry-busters.

(1) Recognise that God cares for birds, flowers, *and you!*

Just picture Jesus as He is saying, "Consider the ravens" just as a flock of birds fly by. Then He points to the wild flowers and uses them as an example of God's care. You may not understand the doctrine of Divine Providence, but you know something about birds and flowers! Even the birds are valuable to God. We love birds at my house. We buy bird seed in bags and have bird feeders. In all my years of watching birds, I've never known a bird to have an ulcer or die from worry. When Jesus spoke of "lilies" He was talking about the wild flowers that spring up and cover the hillsides after a rain. Nobody had to plant them, they just grew and bloomed. There is an important lesson about birds and flowers, but you must stop and dig below the surface. The mum and dad bird work like crazy to build the nest and then to bring food to the baby birds. Baby birds just open their mouths and receive the food, but when they mature, they go out and start working hard for their own food. When Jesus says God will make sure you have food, He doesn't mean you can just sit around and open your mouth or hold out your hand. He wants you to work hard. Birds teach us the importance of diligence. Flowers are beautiful, but they are totally dependent. They can't grow on their own, but they don't worry about it. Flowers can't produce what they need: nutrients, moisture, and light, they can only accept them.

Flowers teach us the importance of dependence. Here's the lesson: We should be as *diligent* as birds and as *dependent* as flowers! Don't worry about food. Work hard like birds and God will make sure you have enough to eat. Don't worry about having clothes to wear. Like the flowers, God will make sure you have something to wear. God didn't promise you'd have gourmet food or designer labels, but He *does* promise He will meet your needs. The flowers and birds are His creation, but we are His children!

So don't worry about your food or clothes! Don't worry - be faithful!

(2) Receive *today* as a gift – Forget *tomorrow's* worries

Jesus knew one of the greatest dangers of worry is that it distracts our attention from *now*. Jesus says exactly that in Matthew 6:34. Here is The Message paraphrase: "Give your entire attention to what God is doing right now, and don't get worked up about what may or may not happen tomorrow. God will help you deal with whatever hard things come up when the time comes."

I've heard worry-holics say something like: "I'm just afraid that something bad is going to happen in the future!" You're correct, something bad IS going to happen to you in the future. Bad things happen to all of us but God is good - all the time. Instead of focusing on bad possibilities of the future focus on the goodness of God today - and forever. It's okay to consider the future and plan wisely for the future, but don't *worry* about the future. Corrie Ten Boom said it well: "Worry does not empty *tomorrow* of its *sorrows;* it empties *today* of its *strength.*"

Psalm 90 teaches us that we are to number our *days* not our *years.* Every day of life is a precious gift of God, so don't let worry about tomorrow ruin your today. Did you hear about the clock that had a nervous breakdown? It ticked once every second. One day it started thinking about the fact it would have to tick 60 times each minute, 360 times each hour, 8,640 times a day, 3,153,600 times a year... and if it ticked five years that would mean 15,768,000 ticks! The clock couldn't stand it so it went to a chronographic psychiatrist - a clock doc. The little clock was all upset. He said, "There's just no way I can tick 15,768,000 times!" The clock doc said, "How many ticks do you have to tick at a time?" The clock said, "Just one." The doc said, "Well, don't worry about the next tick, just think about each tick at a time and you'll be okay." The clock decided to do that, and it left ticking right along. You see, life will give you a beating but you can keep on ticking, if you just think about each tick as it happens!

(3) Reduce anxiety by *simplifying* your life

One reason people worry is because their lives are so complicated. They have so many activities and demands that they can't do everything well, so they worry about it. The busier you get, the more anxious you become. In the story Jesus told about how different kinds of people receive the good seed of the Word of God, He spoke of one type of person who has such a cluttered life that the Word of God can't really produce fruit. Is He describing you when He said in Luke 8:14, "The seed that fell among the thorns stands for those who hear, but as they go on their way they are choked by life's worries, riches, and pleasures, and they do not mature." Have you read Luke 12? Like real estate, scripture is all about location, location, location. If you slip back up to the verses preceding this, Jesus just told the story of a wealthy entrepreneur who had so much he had to tear down his warehouses and build bigger warehouses. But he died before he got to a place of being able to enjoy any of it.

The point Jesus made is in Luke 12:15 where He said, "Watch out for greed. A man's life does not consist of the abundance of his possessions." If there is one message that keeps getting pounded into our heads by our culture, it's "things do matter." The message of our culture is "grab more and more stuff!" It blares from the television commercials; it stares at you from the pages of magazines and newspapers. We are like the donkey that has a carrot extended in front of it on a stick. The donkey sees that carrot and moves toward it, but the carrot just moves away. He is always wanting and pursuing it, but he never gets it.

Here's a great word for the 21st century, try it on for size: *contentment*. People worry because they aren't content; they are always striving for the next level, the next job, the next thrill. A recovering *worry-holic* is someone who has learned the secret of contentment.

I came across an amazing quote from a 14-year-old boy. He demonstrates unusual maturity. It's all about learning to be content.

"It was spring, but it was summer I wanted, the warm days, and the great outdoors.

It was summer, but it was fall I wanted, the colourful leaves, and the cool dry air.

It was autumn, but it was winter I wanted, the beautiful snow, and the joy of the holiday season.

It was winter, but it was spring I wanted, the warmth, and the blossoming of nature.

I was a child, but it was adulthood I wanted. The freedom, and the respect.

I was 20, but it was 30 I wanted, to be mature, and sophisticated.

I was middle-aged, but it was 20 I wanted, the youth and the free spirit.

I was retired, but it was middle age I wanted, the presence of mind, without limitations.

My life was over, but I never got what I wanted."

That's why people worry. They haven't learned the simple secret of contentment.

The apostle Paul wrote in Philippians: "I have learned the secret of being content in any and every situation." We should work hard and always be striving to grow and mature as a Christian. In other words, never be content with your spiritual maturity, but you must learn to be content with what you have. If you don't learn simple contentment, worry will rob you of the joy of *now*.

(4) Refuse to carry your *burdens* alone

We worry about our problems when we try to carry them alone. Many of the burdens we have to carry are far too heavy to bear alone. A wonderful worry-buster is to learn how to unload your burdens.

I love the funny story about the man who had a reputation for being a *worry-holic*. He was always anxious and miserable from worrying. One day he showed up for work and there was an evident transformation in his attitude and countenance. He was smiling and happy as if he didn't have a care in the world. One of his co-workers noticed and said, "Man, what happened to you? You look great!" The former worry-wart said, "Oh, I have hired a professional worrier to do all my worrying for me. It's great. I pay him and he worries for me; anything that I might worry about, he does it." His co-worker said, "That's a great idea! How much do you pay him?" The man said, "I pay him £2,000 a week to worry for me." His co-worker said, "Wait a minute! £2,000 a week? You don't make that much money - how are you going to pay him?" The man said, "That's not *my* worry - it's *his!*"

Wouldn't it be wonderful if you could find someone who would take all your worries? That's exactly what God has offered to do, for free! The Bible says in 1 Peter 5:7: "Cast all your anxiety on Him because He cares for you." What an invitation! We can say, "Lord, I won't worry about this anymore, I'm just going to unload this burden on You." God says, "Go ahead, I'm a lot stronger than you are!" Why do we find that so hard to do? Do we think we're being NICE to the Lord when we insist on carrying our burdens alone?

> *"It is His Will that I should cast my cares on Him each day;*
> *He also bids me not to cast my confidence away.*
> *But, Oh! How foolishly I act when taken unaware,*
> *I cast away my confidence and carry all my care!"*

Right now, if you so choose, you can simply choose to cast your cares on the Lord and you'll feel like a great weight has been lifted off of your shoulders. But sometimes you may need another person to help you carry a load. As the Body of Christ, we *are* the hands, and the shoulders, and the back of the Lord. As brothers and sisters we should be willing to help carry the burdens of others. Paul writes in Galatians: "Carry each other's burdens, and in this way you will fulfil the law of Christ." The law of Christ is to love God and to love your neighbour as yourself. When you offer to support and pray and help someone, you are being the Body of Christ.

(5) Realise that *pleasing* God is all that really matters

Jesus gives us the shortcut to worry-free living in verse 31: "Seek His kingdom, and these things [food, clothes, other needs] will be given to you as well." We worry because we don't think we can live to everyone else's expectations; you don't have to worry about whether or not you can. You can't. Throughout history or literature there have been all different kinds of kingdoms but they all had one important factor in common. Every kingdom has a king. You can't have a kingdom without one. Instead of trying to figure out what the Kingdom of God is, just concentrate on the King, Jesus. The only thing a loyal subject in a kingdom has to do is to *please* the king. If you don't please the king, you are in trouble! You can please King Jesus by loving Him, obeying Him, and serving Him. He is a loving, caring King who has both the inclination and the resources to meet all the needs in your life. So instead of seeking to have all your needs met, seek to honour and please the King. Don't focus on doing a hundred different things, just focus on pleasing God. 200 years from today, none of us will be alive. All these things that you are worrying about today won't matter then. But if you dedicate your life to pleasing God, in 200 years you'll recognise it as the smartest thing you ever decided to do. In a million years, it will be the *only* thing that really matters.

Are you worrying? Don't worry - be faithful! Are you afraid? Don't worry - be faithful! You may be thinking, "If you only knew what I'm going through, you wouldn't be telling me not to worry!" I don't know what you're going through, but God does and He cares. And He is the one telling you not to worry. You say, "Well, He's God, He doesn't have anything to worry about!" Well let's listen to one more voice. There once was a man who had been stoned several times and left for dead, he had been shipwrecked, thrown to wild beasts, and hunted by a vicious mob who wanted to kill him. He was in prison waiting to have his head chopped off. While he was in prison, surrounded by Roman guards, he wrote a letter, and here's one of the things he said: "Do not be anxious about anything, but in everything by prayer and petition with thanksgiving, present your requests to God. And the *peace of God that transcends all understanding,* will guard your hearts and minds in Christ Jesus." If you will refuse to worry and instead seek the King and ask Him for peace, He will give it to you. The world doesn't understand this kind of inner peace, and it only comes from God. But when you have this peace from God, it protects your mind like those Roman guards surrounded Paul.

Life is way too short to waste time worrying.

Bishop Taylor Smith used to quote this little poem:
"The worried cow would have lived 'till now; If she'd only saved her breath;
But she feared her hay wouldn't last all day and she mooed herself to death."

Don't waste your life worrying! Life only has two handles. When the difficulties and challenges of life confront you, you can grab the handle of worry and fear. Or you can grab the handle of faith and trust. You can't grab both handles at the same time. Will you say, "Lord, today, I will let go of the handle of worry and fear and I will start taking the handle of faith with both hands and *I will not let go* of my faith and trust in You. From this day forward my motto will be 'Don't worry - be faithful!' "

Chapter 11
When Good People Suffer

I've preached on suffering several times. In fact, one lady wrote me a note reading, "Derek, I never knew what suffering was until I heard you preach. *Now I know.*" Some preaching is like suffering. Once a long-winded preacher had been going about an hour and didn't seem anywhere close to ending. He said, "I'm really on a roll here, and there's a lot more that I want to say, but Jesus has just told me to stop, so let's end the service. Jesus has told me to end my message." The worship leader said, "Let's stand and sing, *'What a friend we have in Jesus'.*"

This is a chapter about terrorists and falling towers. Bombs on our streets, buses and train stations. People were going about their business when they were suddenly and brutally killed. Why were those innocent people killed? Where was God during all of that? Most of you think I'm writing about 9:11, and similar events since then. Everything I've said does apply to that, but I'm really talking about 13:1. Luke 13:1.

2,000 years ago, Jesus talked about some innocent people who died at the hands of what could be called terrorists - and He talked about a tower that fell and killed people. In fact, the similarities between 13:1 and 9:11 are amazing. The same questions people are asking today were being asked 2,000 years ago. But more importantly, the answer Jesus gives is the same answer we need to hear.

"Now there were some present at the time who told Jesus about the Galileans whose blood Pilate had mixed with their sacrifices. Jesus answered, "Do you think that these Galileans were worse sinners than all the other Galileans because they suffered this way? I tell you, no! But unless you repent, you too will all perish. Or those eighteen who died when the tower in Siloam fell on them - do you think they were more guilty than all the others living in

Jerusalem? I tell you, no! But unless you repent, you too will all perish." Then He relayed this parable: "A man had a fig tree, planted in his vineyard, and he went to look for fruit on it, but did not find any. So he said to the man who took care of the vineyard, 'For three years now I've been coming to look for fruit on this fig tree and haven't found any. Cut it down! Why should it use up the soil?' 'Sir,' the man replied, 'leave it alone for one more year, and I'll dig around it and fertilise it. If it bears fruit next year, fine! If not, then cut it down'." (Luke 13;1-9).

The Holy Spirit of Jesus is present with us today, but if He was here in the flesh, we could sit down in front of Him and ask, "Jesus, what about those passengers who were killed on those hijacked airliners? And what about those people killed when the World Trade Centre was attacked all those years ago? And while we're on the subject, what about those people killed in the Madrid bombing and the London bombing of course. And then there's the Middle East and... we could go on. You may not like Jesus' answer, or His non-answer. You come with a deep, troubling philosophical question, "Why do good people suffer?" and He basically refuses to answer it; instead He turns the question into a statement about your own spiritual condition. A conversation with Jesus is never boring!

Christianity and the Bible can easily endure the light of honest intellectual scrutiny; it has for 20 centuries. So, you don't have to check your brain at the door when you go to church. This idea of suffering has puzzled us for centuries. There is an entire theological or philosophical study called *theodicy.* It asks the simple question: If God is entirely good, and entirely powerful - why is there suffering? Some people look at what the Bible says about God and then look around in the world and say, "The character of God and the reality of suffering contradict each other!" What's the answer?

Have you read Robinson Crusoe by Daniel Defoe? It is a deeply spiritual book because Defoe was a committed Christian who wrote hymns and Christian poetry. When Defoe's character, Robinson Crusoe, is shipwrecked on an island, he discovers a native and names him Friday. He teaches him to speak English and he teaches him about God and about the importance of trusting Jesus Christ for salvation. In one of their theological discussions, the following dialogue occurs:

Friday to Robinson Crusoe:
"But if God much strong, much more than devil, why God no kill the devil so make him no more do evil?"

Crusoe's reply:
"You may as well ask, why God no kill you and me when we do wicked things"

That short conversation provides both the question and a good response to the problem of theodicy, the question of, "How can a loving, powerful God allow evil?" Let's learn four important things about suffering.

First: Suffering is part of a fallen world

There was no suffering in the Garden of Eden. But when our ancestors, Adam and Eve chose to disobey a loving God, suffering became a reality. We are still living in a world affected by the results of sin. After a nuclear explosion, "fallout" lingers for many years. Even, so we are still living in the "fallout" from the fall of man. God is not the source of evil; Satan and sin are responsible.

Human suffering is produced from two different sources, both of which Jesus addresses in Luke 13.

(1) We live in a world full of MORAL EVIL.

We have to share this planet with some wicked people. Pilate was a cruel Roman governor. One day some Galileans were in the Temple getting ready to make their sacrifices. Pilate did not trust the Jews, so he had Roman soldiers disguised as Jews to intermingle with them. For some unknown reason, on a certain day, Pilate gave the order to massacre a group of worshippers. The Jews were still outraged that Pilate would mingle the blood of the worshippers with their sacrifices. The world has always had to deal with cruel, wicked people like Pilate. Whether it's

Hitler ordering the death of six million Jews, or the gunman rushing into a shopping centre, or the misguided religious zeal of terrorists. This world is just full of mean people.

The Bible speaks of the depravity of the human heart. We read in Jeremiah, "The heart is deceitful above all things and beyond cure. Who can understand it?" Jesus said, "For from within, out of men's hearts, come evil thoughts, sexual immorality, theft, murder, adultery..." Look no further than your pocket or purse. If you have any kind of a key with you today, it is a testimony to the fact we have to lock things up, or some mean person will steal your car or your possessions. The heart of the human problem is the problem of the human heart. Man is basically a sinner who has to have a life-transforming encounter with God to become a better person. Don't blame God for the actions of wicked people. When God created us, He gave us the freedom to choose, and some people choose to commit acts of evil and violence.

(2) Another source of suffering is that we also live in a world of NATURAL EVIL.

Sometimes we suffer and it's not because of some wicked person, it could be what we call accidents and disasters. You could even include disease in this category. Why are there tornadoes, earthquakes, or accidents in which people are hurt or die? Why is there cancer, infection, and disease? It's because we live in a fallen, messed up world. When Adam and Eve sinned, they opened a Pandora's box of troubles for them and for their descendants.

Have you ever heard the world's shortest poem? It's called "Troubles" and here's the poem:
"Troubles–
Adam had 'em!"
He had plenty of troubles - and so do we.

Several years ago the World Trade Center Towers fell because of evil men flying fuel-laden jetliners into them. We don't really know why the tower of Siloam fell; we just know 18 people died. Perhaps it was human error - it wasn't built well. Or perhaps it's one of the unavoidable accidents occurring in life. Romans 8:22 says, "We know that the whole creation has been groaning as in the pains of childbirth right up to the present time." This is a beautiful world in many ways - the spacious skies, the amber waves of grain; the purple mountain's majesty... but it is also a world that is not perfect. The Bible says the very creation itself has been whacked out of kilter; you can almost hear it groaning like a woman in pain. Creation isn't running right because of sin. One day, creation itself will be fixed and redeemed but for the time being we have to live in an imperfect world where there are storms, accidents, and disease. Don't blame God: we messed it up.

Have you ever cleaned up your house in preparation for receiving guests or visitors and when they arrive, they begin to mess up your house? You know it's a good house; it's just been messed up by these visitors. This can be annoying! Now think about how God feels about mankind messing up His perfect Creation!" This leads to a Second principle.

Second: Suffering is unrelated to goodness

The question in the minds of Jesus' audience was, "Why did those people suffer and die from Pilate's cruelty or from the tower falling?" The assumption was they must have been bad people to suffer like that. There is a tendency for us to look at someone when they are suffering and to think, "Maybe they are just getting what they deserve."

In John 9, Jesus was walking along when he saw a blind man. His disciples asked Him, "Master who sinned? This man or his parents that he was born blind?" Don't we sometimes think the same way? What did this person do to deserve their suffering? Pay attention to what Jesus told His disciples, "Neither this man nor his parents sinned that he was born blind, but this happened that the work of God might be displayed in his life."

We still make the same false assumption today. Jesus asks, "Do you think those upon whom the tower fell were worse sinners than you? No!" That kind of thinking assaults our sense of fairness or justice. We think bad people should be the ones to suffer and good people shouldn't. But that's not the way it works. Why do good people suffer? It's actually not a very good question, because none is good in the first place!

Once a man approached Jesus and called Him "good." Notice Jesus' reply in Luke 18 "Why do you call me good?" Jesus answered. "No one is good – except God alone." The Psalmist says, "There is none good - no not one." God is good all the time, but I don't think any of us can claim that designation for ourselves. I'm a sinner saved by grace. We want to know why bad things happen to good people; we're asking the wrong question. In effect what Jesus was saying was this: "You people are asking the wrong question. You should be asking me, 'Why didn't that tower fall on MY head?'"

Maybe you've pondered the mystery of, "Why do bad things happen to good people?" Have you ever stopped to wonder, "Why do good things happen to bad people - like me?" Suffering is no respecter of persons, at one time everyone will suffer - the good, the bad, the ugly. In fact, the Bible promises those who follow Christ *will* suffer. But the good news is that any suffering we endure in this world is only temporary. The Bible says in Romans 8, "We share in his sufferings in order that we may also share in his glory. I consider that our present sufferings are not worthy to be compared with the glory that will be revealed in us." Yes, we will suffer in this life - but this life is not all there is!

I recall a TV sitcom years ago which actually addressed this matter in one of its episodes. To the best of my recollection, here's the dialogue:
One man says: *"Tell me, if there is a God, why is this world messed up?"*
Another responds: *"Why do I always have to give the answers?"*
Turning to a friend he says, *"Tell this idiot why, if God has created the world, it's in such a mess?"*
The lady says: *"Well, I suppose it's to make us appreciate heaven better when we get there."*

In the midst of a funny show, the writers actually wrote something profound in the script. There will be NO suffering in heaven. Do you know for certain you'll spend eternity there? Here's how you can be certain. This is the third principle we need to grasp:

Third: Suffering amplifies God's message: "repent or perish!"

When asked why Pilate killed the people or why the 18 died when the tower fell, Jesus gave the same reply twice: "unless you repent you will likewise perish." Go ahead, ask Him again, "Jesus, why are there terrorists who steal aeroplanes and bring towers crashing down? Why do they bomb our streets, trains and buses?" He would tell you, "Wrong question - but unless you repent, you will also perish!" That's His message: *repent or perish!*

Every person is born with an instinct to worship, to relate to Someone greater and more powerful than the human species. Consequently, man has devised a wide range of gods and deities and worshipped in many different ways. When God sent Jesus, He was sending the final, authoritative revelation of Himself. Once, Paul was speaking to a group of intellectual giants in Athens. He had seen all their statues and gods - and they had one unnamed shrine that simply said, "to the unknown God." Paul took it as an opportunity to tell them that the "unknown God" was the true God - and His name is Jesus. Paul said: "In the past God overlooked... ignorance, but now He commands all men everywhere to repent. For He has set a day when He will judge the world by the man He has appointed. He has given proof of this to all men by raising Him from the dead."

The Resurrection of Jesus was God's stamp of approval on the Deity of Jesus. To repent means to change your mind, and then change your behaviour. It's a word that means to turn. If you are driving down the road and a passenger said, "turn right," you might choose to turn the steering wheel to the right and change direction. That's a good picture of the Bible word for "repent." You change your mind about your direction and then you change your direction. To repent means you turn from sin, and you turn to Jesus. Repentance is not a single action; it is a lifestyle. We must be continually repenting throughout our lives if we want to be right with God. When I read in the Bible that I'm thinking a way the Bible says is wrong, I need to repent immediately. If I read in the Bible that I should be doing something I'm not doing, I need to repent and start doing it. Repentance is not easy because the first step in repentance is admitting you are wrong - and that is not a natural human tendency. Most of us have being right down to an art.

God uses many tools to call us to repentance, even our suffering. C. S. Lewis wrote: *"Pain insists upon being attended to; God whispers to us in our pleasures, speaks in our conscience, but shouts in our pains: it is His megaphone to rouse a deaf world."* When everything is going wonderfully in your life, you may not think you need God. But suffering gets our attention and reminds us that we cannot make it without God.

Some of you are suffering right now. You aren't suffering because you are a worse sinner than the rest of us. And some of you are doing great right now, no complaints. That doesn't mean you are better than the person near you who is hurting. Now God doesn't create evil or suffering, but He will certainly use the suffering that is a part of this fallen world to call you to repent. Is there something you need to change your mind about today, and then change your behaviour? God may be shouting to you, Repent! Repent!" Are you listening? One final thought:

Fourth: God is extending your grace period another day!

On the surface, you may think the little story about the fig tree is unrelated to what Jesus is saying about suffering and repentance but He uses it as a powerful story to illustrate His point. The owner of the farm is God, and the fig tree is Israel. God is ready to cut the fig tree down, because for three years there is no fruit but He decides to give it another season to see if it will become fruitful. You can't miss the point. Jesus had been preaching for three years, and within a few months, He would go to the cross. Israel had not yet become fruitful in accepting the Messiah, so God was giving them a longer period to repent and accept Jesus. The message is the same to us today. If you haven't trusted Jesus as your Saviour yet, God is giving you another chance to surrender to Him.

Some insurance policies have what is called a "grace period." If you don't pay your premium on time, the insurance company extends your coverage for a short period of time, hoping you'll pay the premium. But if you don't pay the premium, the grace period runs out and the policy will be cancelled. God has a grace period, too, and you're in it today. We are living in the age of grace today. Salvation is absolutely free - but there is a limit to your grace period. You are facing a Divine Deadline. It could be one of two deadlines: you could die unexpectedly and that's the end of your grace period, or Jesus could come suddenly and rapture the church. At that point, your grace period runs out.

Like the old preacher said, "You are either going to meet the undertaker, or the upper-taker, but either way, you'd better be ready to meet God!" If you are not a Christian, God is giving you an extension to your grace period. He allowed you to wake up today. Right now, He can promise you forgiveness and eternal life but He doesn't promise you another chance tomorrow. You may not live until tomorrow - or Jesus could return at any moment. People sometimes say, "It's never too late." When it comes to accepting God's grace, it can be too late. You are like the fig tree. God is showing you His grace and patience by giving you another chance to become fruitful in Christ.

The Bible says in 2 Peter: "God isn't late with His promise as some measure lateness. He is restraining Himself on account of you, holding back the End because He doesn't want anyone lost. He's giving everyone space and time to change. But when the Day of God's Judgement does come, it will be unannounced, like a thief." The most important question you'll ever ask is not "Why do good people suffer?" The most important question is "Am I ready to meet God?" Or "Where will I spend eternity?"

Chapter 12
When You Lose Your Way

"The Lord delights in the way of the man whose steps he has made firm; though he stumble, he will not fall, for the Lord upholds him with his hand" (Psalm 37:23-24)

"Though he stumble." Some translations say, "When he falls." Note that it does not say, "If he stumbles." There is a big difference between "when" and "if". The latter states a probability; the former declares a certainty. David understood that all believers fall eventually. We stumble, we lose our way, we struggle. No one is exempt. We all fall sooner or later. It's what happens when we stumble along that makes all the difference.

We can summarise the teaching of this text in two simple statements.

(1) God ordains every step we take - the good and the bad, the happy and the sad, the positive and the negative.

The verb "made firm" is very strong in the original Hebrew. It means to establish something so that it has a strong foundation. Proverbs 16:9 tells us that "in his heart a man plans his course, but the LORD determines his steps." Same idea. Most of us know that God "directs" our steps. But this verb is even stronger. God not only "directs" our steps, He also "determines" or "ordains" our steps. Because He is God, there are no accidents with Him. No circumstance - whether good or bad - can come to us apart from God's determined purpose for us.

All of us wonder what the next few months will bring. What will happen? Will it be a good time or a bad time for us personally? I've researched that question diligently and I know the answer: The next few months will be a lot like the last few months. In some ways, it will be business as usual.

You'll have good days and bad days. You will have some victories and some defeats. You'll be sick for a while and you'll be healthy much of the time. Some of your prayers will be answered; some won't be answered. Some of your dreams will come true; some will be dashed on the rocks of hard reality. You'll discover that some of your friends will be there when you need them. Others will fail you when you need them most. In many respects, life will be the same next week because we all face the same ongoing challenges in our walk with the Lord. But know this: Your steps in coming weeks are "made firm" by the Lord. He is in charge of the details of your life.

(2) God promises that when we fall, we will not be utterly destroyed.

Let's read the beginning of verse 23 of Psalm 37 again - "Though he stumbles, he will not fall." Picture a trail that winds through a dense forest. As the person walks forward, he doesn't see the rock buried just beneath the surface, and so he trips and falls to the ground. Life is like that. We all stumble in many ways. The word translated "utterly destroyed" means to be cast headlong into a deep pit. It's what happens when you stand at a cliff edge peering over the edge, looking down 500 feet, when someone pushes you from behind. When you finally hit bottom, you won't dust yourself off and keep on going. You've been "utterly destroyed."

God promises that won't happen to you and me. Though we may face desperate, life-changing circumstances next year, God will not allow us to be utterly destroyed. Nothing can happen that will sever our relationship with Him. The reason is clear. He upholds us with His mighty hand. Think of a father walking along with his young son by his side. There are two ways father and son might hold hands. The young boy may reach up with his tiny hand to grasp his father's huge hand. That works until the child stumbles and he is forced to let go of his father's hand. But if the father places his huge hand around his son's tiny hand, the boy is safe no matter what happens because his father's hand holds him up. He may stumble but the father's hand "upholds" him.

The "fall" may be a fall into trouble or catastrophe, or it may be a fall into serious moral sin. The fall might be occasioned by the loss of a job, a health problem, the break-up of a marriage, the end of a friendship, bankruptcy, or any sort of personal crisis that causes the loss of your reputation. Or it could be a series of foolish choices that led you in a wrong direction so that you hurt your walk with God and hurt those around you as well.

Sometimes the "fall" of circumstances causes a "fall" into bitterness, substance abuse, anger, rage, abusive speech, foolish decisions, lust, adultery, or other bad actions. The Bible repeatedly shows how easily this can happen to even the best people. The Bible tells us the whole truth about human nature. We see men and women who are faithful one day and fickle the next. We see Peter boasting, and then he is busted by his own sin. We see worship mixed with worry, courage followed by cowardice, faith matched with doubt, generosity followed by greed, kindness overcome by arrogance. We learn that strong people sometimes do very stupid things. Saints often act like sinners.

These stories are in the Bible both to instruct us and to encourage us. They teach us that even the best men under pressure can do very foolish things. No one is beyond the reach of temptation. Very godly people can make some very wrong choices - and suffer greatly as a result. And cause others to suffer with them. It's good that the Bible shows this to us - or we would be tempted to deny this reality. We like to think, "I'm beyond that temptation." Don't ever say that. You don't know what you're *"beyond"*. Today's "victory" may actually set you up for tomorrow's "defeat". Satan roams the world like a mighty lion, looking for over-confident Christians he can devour.

Signposts on life's way.

Here are two other verses we should consider. Proverbs 24:16, "Though a righteous man falls seven times, he rises again, but the wicked are brought down by calamity." We may fall again and again, trouble may come again and again, we may struggle again and again - and again! But it is the Lord's purpose that we should rise - again and again and again. Psalm 145:14 declares that, "The Lord upholds all those who fall and lifts up all who are bowed down."

When you fall, remember this: God never intends you to stay down forever. He intends for you to "rise up" and keep on walking with Him. So what does this mean? What practical help is there in knowing all of this. You say, "Life hurts... or it may do very soon. What's the application of this truth?" Here are four practical applications.

(1) Every detail of life is under God's control.

If God is God, then He must know about all the things that happen to us, and in some sense we can't fully understand, that "all things" includes both the best and the worst that comes our way. A thought that may come to us here is this - Does this mean even our sins are "ordered" by the Lord. We have to think carefully in answering a question like this. God is never the author or instigator of sin. Never. Sin is always our own responsibility. But that does not fully answer the question. If our sin can somehow exist independently of God so that our sin (and indeed, all the sin and misery of the universe) can somehow exist outside of God's eternal plan, then God cannot truly be sovereign over all parts of the universe.

We might ask the question this way: Is God sovereign over Satan? The answer must be "yes!" When you come all the way to the bottom line, the answer goes something like this: God reigns over all parts of the universe all the time, and He does it in such a way that all things must fit into His eternal plan. This even includes the reality of sin itself. For reasons that we only partly understand, God decreed to permit sin to enter the universe (primarily to display His glory through the grace that would be shown in redeeming sinners through the death of His Son, the Lord Jesus Christ). When we sin, we remain fully accountable for the wrong choices we make - and the negative consequences we must face. But if God did not allow it to happen, it would not happen. Thus in the broadest sense of God's sovereignty, even our sin cannot take place apart from God's divine decree.

150

People speak of this as being a mystery. Absolutely, and it is a mystery so enormous that we will spend eternity learning more about it, and marvelling at the riches of God's grace and the wisdom of His plan. But if this is not true, then God is not truly God at all, and we are (to borrow an Apostle Paul phrase) of all men most miserable. But it is true, and therefore we rejoice to serve a God whose ways are far beyond our limited minds to understand. He can make the wrath of man praise Him. There is an important personal application to be made at this point. Since every detail of life comes under God's control, we can remain confident and peaceful even when life itself seems to spin out of control.

Are you familiar with the name George Muller of Bristol? There's a road (a long one) named after him in Bristol. For over 60 years, George Muller directed an orphanage in Bristol, England, that provided for over 10,000 boys and girls. Here is the amazing fact: He never once made an appeal for money. He depended on God for whatever was needed to support the work. He would gather with his fellow workers to cry out to God for help. On many occasions, the help came while they prayed - a grocer would come by with bread, cheese, meat and eggs so the children would have breakfast in the morning. Mr. Muller proved in his own life that you can take God at his Word. After he died, someone picked up his well-worn Bible and began to leaf through it. Because Mr. Muller was an avid Bible reader, its pages were filled with jottings from his daily devotions. Next to the words of Psalm 37:23, he had added two little words to the text: "The steps *and stops* of a good man are ordered by the Lord." How true that is. For the Christian the path of life is never an unbroken straight line to heaven. We all go through "many dangers, toils and snares" on our way to the Heavenly City. How good to know that our God ordains both the steps *and stops* of life.

(2) God takes pleasure in our struggle to walk in holiness.

"The Lord delights in the ways of the man." Consider a father and his young daughter who is just learning how to walk. For months she has been crawling; recently she has learned how to pull herself up and stand on her wobbling legs while holding her father's hand. One day she pulls her hand free, wobbles for a moment, tries to take a step forward, and falls down. Does her father tell her off for falling down? Of course not. He smiles a bit at her tears, and then he helps her back up. Good parents know that falling is a necessary part of learning how to walk. If you never fall, you'll never learn how to walk. And parents do their children no favours by being so protective that their children never fall down. Falling isn't fun for the child, but a wise parent knows that falling always comes before walking. This applies directly to the "falls" we take spiritually. Our struggles are necessary even though they are not pleasant or easy to endure. Sometimes (often!) we bring trouble on ourselves by the foolish choices we make. And sometimes we end up hurting ourselves and those around us very greatly by repeating those bad choices over and over again. Marriages end, friendships are broken, churches split, our children suffer, and the cause of Christ is hurt by the things we say and do. Sin is serious business, and we never sin without hurting ourselves, and very often, those around us.

I don't mean to suggest that God takes pleasure in our sin or that our sin does not bring punishment. But when we sin, we sometimes wrongly conclude that "God must hate me now." And in our despair we want to hide in a closet and never come out. How could God ever take us back after what we did? The answer is, God loves His children with an everlasting love. Nothing we say or do can ever separate us from the love of God in Christ Jesus. We are joined to our Father with bands of eternal love stronger than steel. He loves us too much to let us go on in sin forever. And when we turn back to Him, with trembling lips, deeply guilty, fearing the worst, thinking all hope is lost, we discover the good news that He waits with open arms for us to come home to Him.

When the Prodigal Son finally came to his senses in the "far country," having wasted his inheritance on riotous living so that he ended up eating with the pigs, having rehearsed what he would say, feeling no longer worthy to be called his father's son, in the midst of his shame and despair, trudging down the long road home - after all that, when he was "yet a long way off," his father ran to meet him, hugged him, and smothered him with kisses.

When your children disobey and you punish them, do you hate them or do you love them? You discipline them because you love them and because your heart is broken over their disobedience. The same is true a million times more of our heavenly Father. The things we suffer because of our disobedience prove that God still loves us. He waits anxiously for the slightest turn in our direction. No matter what we have done, if we will return to the Lord, He will abundantly pardon us. God "permits" us to fall when He could stop it. If He permits it, then what He permits must ultimately be for our spiritual benefit. Not the fall itself, but what we will eventually learn from it. God "allows" us to suffer when He could stop it. Not that suffering itself is good, but it is often the pathway to enormous blessing for us.

(3) God designs our trials so they will not destroy us.

This follows from all that I have said. Verse 24 assures us that though we may "stumble" or "fall" temporarily, we will not be utterly destroyed. God will not allow anything to permanently destroy our relationship with Him. Not even death itself can sever our strong connection with God.

Job 23:10, "He knows the way that I take; when he has tested me, I will come forth as gold." When you are "in the furnace", it is hard to believe that any good could result from the fiery trial, but God says, "Wait for a while and you will see pure gold." During the worst moments, we take this by faith and hang on to God, believing that better days must eventually come. Thus it is that Job lost everything. Joseph was cast into prison on a phoney rape charge, and Jonah ended up in the belly of a great fish. Jonah was a very reluctant prophet whose final words are both angry and accusing. But still he was God's man for Nineveh. God said, "I'm going to send you to the belly of a fish so you can think about things for a while." He did, and eventually he was puked out on the beach (not a very pleasant experience). Job lost everything and gained back more than he lost.

Joseph ended up the second most powerful man in Egypt. Sometimes our trials lead to a promotion; other times we feel like we've been puked up on the beach. God does it both ways - and we'll probably experience both if we live long enough. But God had bigger things in mind in all three cases. He wasn't through with Job or Joseph or Jonah. Nor is He through with us just because we stumble and fall.

Consider what Jesus said to Peter in the Upper Room on the night before He was crucified: "Satan has asked to sift you as wheat. But I have prayed for you, that your faith may not fail. And when you have turned back, strengthen your brothers." This statement deserves special notice because Jesus said it before Peter's threefold denial. In fact, Jesus said it just before Peter made his boastful promise of unending faithfulness. The point is, Jesus saw it all coming, knew everything before it took place: The boasting, The teenage girl around the fire, The swearing, The repeated denials, The shame, The bitter tears, The guilt, The restoration. He knew Peter better than Peter knew himself. He knew the "steps" Peter was about to take in the wrong direction. In a sense, He had more genuine confidence in Peter than Peter had in himself. By himself, Peter was just full of himself. But Jesus said, "I have prayed for you." He didn't stop Peter from boasting or from denying. He let matters take their natural course, but He prayed for Peter, knowing that Peter at heart was a good man who loved Him, and knowing that his denial was not the "real" Peter. The "real" Peter was the man who declared, "You are the Christ, the Son of the living God." Jesus allowed Peter to fall away, knowing that through His prayers, Peter would eventually return, and when he did, he would be a better, stronger man, humbled by his failure, ready to serve the Lord with a humility born of painful failure.

Let's review the first three applications:
1) Every detail of life is under God's control.
2) God takes pleasure in our struggle to walk in holiness.
3) God designs our trials so they will not destroy us.
Which brings us to the next application -

(4) We will not utterly fall because God will not let go.

154

Theologians call this the doctrine of eternal security. It simply means that those whom God saves, He saves forever. Though we stumble and fall a thousand times, God's love is firm because His purposes are eternal. Our salvation rests not on our performance but on God's unchanging character.

Let me quote Charles Spurgeon: "No saint shall fall finally or fatally. Sorrow may bring us to the earth, and death may bring us to the grave, but lower we cannot sink, and out of the lowest of all we shall arise to the highest of all."

Martin Luther said that it takes three things to make a man of God - meditation, prayer and temptation. We're fine with the first two because we know we need to read the Bible and pray. But most of us would not add "temptation" to the list. Luther meant that godly character can only be developed in the crucible of life where we fight many battles with the world, the flesh, and the devil. The temptation to quit, to despair, to give in to bitterness, to flee the struggle, to yield to lust, to give in to greed, to indulge ourselves, to walk in pride, these things either destroy us or they make us stronger. Prayer and Bible reading alone cannot make us godly. We need the struggles of life to make us strong.

One Minister made this comment. Looking back on his life he was very sure of himself in his twenties. But he said, "I have bumped up against the hard edge of my limitations and sin, again and again. I am less sure about what's wrong with Christendom, and more sure about what's wrong with me." Those are wise words from a man who has experienced the grace of God through the ups and downs of life.

We do not pretend that our trials never happened or that Christians never suffer. We suffer just like everyone else on this sin-cursed planet. Nor is it good when we fall into sin. Just ask any Christian who fell into serious moral sin how "good" it was. Sin only delights "for a season". All Satan's apples have worms. But there is an important truth in our passage that we need to understand: God is at work in our trials and in our falls in a way we never dreamed, never knew, and never saw at the time. Nothing is wasted with God. All things truly do "work together" for our good and for God's glory - even though we rarely see that in advance.

I remember visiting a man in hospital. He told me that he had less than a year to live. In fact he had less than a month! He said, "I had known that was a possibility, but it is still jolting to hear it said." I saw no bitterness or anger there, and no fear either. My friend wanted to live as long as he could, and he fought as hard as he could, but if you had asked him, "Are you ok?" he'd reply, "Yes, I'm okay." It's not easy but my friend had come to grips with the fact that God loves him and is ordering every step he takes. That's what this great truth can do for us.

Pray for yourself that the truth of these verses will really go home and strengthen you now and for future days. Pray for the people around you in your life too. Pray for me. Prayer is a strength to our soul. Some of the answers we can see. Others are known only to God. I mention that to point out that the prayers of the believers are one way the Lord "upholds" His children as they walk the path that leads from earth to heaven.

Encouragement when life is tough.

Here's a thought that may encourage you. If it is possible, God loves you even more when you struggle because that's when you need Him most. When is a father most honoured? When his children are in trouble and turn to him for help. Even so, our God is honoured and shows His special care for His children when they go through struggles on earth.

Your struggles are necessary – *fight on!*
Your Father has not forgotten you – *hang on!*
Your future is assured – *walk on!*

God will not put you in an unbearable situation. But He may put you in a situation that seems unbearable so that you will turn to Him. Remember that God does not give His strength in advance but only when needed. Each day you will have what you need. We may therefore go forth into the coming days with confidence, hope, and joy.

In the end we come back to the Lord Jesus and back to the cross.
If you are tired of your sin, run to the cross.
If you want a new start in life, run to the cross.
If you feel like a failure, run to the cross.
If you fear the future, run to the cross.
If you need hope and encouragement, run to the cross.
If you want to meet Jesus, run to the cross.

I said earlier in this chapter that the next few months will be just like the last few months. Let me amend that statement just a bit: The next few months will be just like the last few months - only entirely different! Some things will be the same, much will be different, and some things will be brand new to us. Be encouraged. The future rests in the good hands of a God who loves you more than you can imagine. You may stumble, but you won't completely fall. This is God's promise to you.

Chapter 13
Combating The Future Without Fear

On the 1980's TV cop show, "Hill Street Blues," the Sergeant ended the daily roll call with the trademark line, "Hey, let's be careful out there!" Being much younger at the time, the warning didn't mean much, but it means so much more now. There really is a dangerous world out there and a wise person will take precautions to guard against putting life and limb at risk.

The future without fear

What a subject! It touches us all at some time. It is something to be conquered *but also* combated. Repeatedly the Bible tells us that people who were to be used by God in some great way had to be reminded, *"Do not be afraid"*. Mary, the mother of Jesus, on being told that she would bear a Son by the will of God, had to be reminded, "Do not be afraid". Joseph, who would marry her after learning of her pregnancy had to be told by an angel, "Do not be afraid!" When Jesus commissioned the disciples to change the world, He also reminded them of the necessity of courage saying, "Do not be afraid, of those who want to kill you. They can only kill the body; they cannot do any more to you." Peter, fearful of the 'ghost' he saw walking on the water, heard His master's voice saying, "Courage, it's me. Don't be afraid." Peter, suddenly bold, said, "Master, if it's really you, call me to come to you on the water." He said, "Come ahead." Jumping out of the boat, Peter walked on the water to Jesus." Take courage. Turn and face those things that threaten. Sense the Presence of the Master with you - in this moment - and do the impossible for Him.

During a time of economic depression, the American President, Franklin Roosevelt said to a frightened nation, *"We have nothing to fear but fear itself."* He meant

159

unhealthy, unreasonable fear only aggravates a bad situation.

We saw fear etched on the faces of those running from terrorism in our streets. Fear feeds fear - and insidious fear is drifting across our nation like an early morning fog over a lake. Some children are afraid they aren't safe in their bedrooms. We've told our children there is no monster under the bed - only to see again there are monsters that kill innocent civilians. People are afraid about what will happen to our fragile economy.

I write about how to deal with your fear. I want to bring a positive, uplifting message so we can all face the future without fear.

Think about what causes fear today.

Jesus is here in the person of His Holy Spirit. As we read these words from Luke 12 and verse 4, I want you to hear Him speaking these words to you. I want you to imagine Jesus is sitting in front of you and He places His nail scarred hand on your head. "I tell you, my friends, *do not be afraid* of those who kill the body and after that can do no more. But I will show you whom you should fear: Fear him who, after the killing of the body, has power to throw you into hell. Yes, I tell you, fear him. Are not five sparrows sold for two pennies? Yet not one of them is forgotten by God. Indeed the very hairs of your head are all numbered. *don't be afraid;* you are worth more than many sparrows."

Jesus recognised unhealthy fear was dangerous. He predicted in the last days, "men would faint with terror, apprehensive on what is coming on the world." The King James Version translates it this way, "Men's heart would be failing from fear." Indeed, as we stand on the brink of so much international uncertainty, how are we going to face the future without fear? In this passage, Jesus says twice, "Do not be afraid." Then He gives four reasons why you don't have to live in fear, even if the future seems unclear.

First: You don't have to be afraid when you know that: God is more powerful than your enemies.

Jesus is telling us we don't have to fear any human enemy because the worst they can do is to kill the body. Fear of death is real, but Jesus made it clear life is more than this physical existence: You and I also have an eternal soul. So we don't have to be afraid of the worst any human enemy can do to us.

We must confess the words of David when he wrote in the Psalm 56: "When I am afraid, I will trust in you. In God, whose word I praise, in God I trust; I will not be afraid. What can mortal man do to me?" Who is our enemy? During World War II we knew who our enemy was. Terrorism is much harder to identify. These enemies don't use a frontal attack where they can be seen, they slip in and out and cause as much destruction and pain as possible. Even in the light of this new kind of enemy, we don't have to fear. Why? Because our God is more powerful than any enemy. The worst any man can do to us is to kill the body. The enemies of Jesus did it to Him. They tortured Him and nailed Him to a cross, but they couldn't kill Him because there was more to Jesus than just a body: He possessed an eternal soul. And so do we. Instead of fearing any man, we should have a holy awe and reverence toward the powerful, Almighty God. Because HE has power to even cast a soul into hell. No man can send you to hell, nor can any man keep you from going to heaven, only God has that power.

You don't have to cringe in fear before God, because He is a loving Father. But you must respect His awesome power. Don't let the pictures of those jets crashing into buildings scare you, or suicide bombers on our streets. Instead, tremble when you think God is a God of perfect Justice, who says, "Vengeance is mine, says the Lord." Some of those self-deceived extremists killed themselves thinking they would wake up in Paradise with Allah rewarding their martyrdom. Boy, were they surprised! These murderers now find themselves facing an awesome God who hates hands that shed innocent blood.

Terrorists may be able to hide from us but they can't hide from God Almighty. I tremble when I think of His mighty power. It makes me not the least bit afraid of terrorists. In fact, the more you fear God, the less you will fear these enemies. When the great Scottish preacher John Knox was lowered into his grave, it was said of him, "Here lies a man who feared God so much that he never feared the face of any man."

Second: You don't have to be afraid because God cares and He is with you when you face danger.

As people watch replay after replay of terrorist attacks, they may be asking two questions: "Doesn't God care?" and "Where is God?" Jesus spoke about how much God cares for a tiny sparrow. We know from Matthew 10 that two sparrows were sold for one penny, and here it is five for two pennies, meaning the merchant often threw in one for free. In other words, the fifth sparrow was basically valueless - and yet God still watches over that tiny bird. Sometimes you may feel you aren't very valuable or God doesn't really care for you. Jesus said you are more valuable to God than many sparrows. Like Ethel Waters used to sing so eloquently,
"If His eye is on the Sparrow,
I know He watches over me!"

Sparrows are such plentiful, tiny, insignificant creatures. Surely one can be born and fly and die without anyone ever noticing it! We may not notice it, but Jesus said in Matthew 10: God notices every time a tiny sparrow falls dead to the ground. That's how much God cares. And surely He was caring and noticing as innocent people have died. He notices and He cares. God can pay attention to every sparrow and every person at the same time. He has a different attention span than we do. There is no *Divine Attention Deficit Disorder.*

Maybe you've wondered, "Where was God when all those people were dying?" He was in the same place He was when His Son was dying. And He will be with you when you face the most dangerous times of your life. Again, David said, "Even though I walk through the valley of the shadow of death, I will fear no evil, for you are with me." What we see when we watch the TV news night after night is the unadulterated face of pure evil - but we don't have to fear any evil, because God cares and God is there. I expect there to be other acts of violence and evil unleashed on our population but don't be afraid, God is with you. Whatever danger you may face, God is there to give you strength.

I once read a story about a tribe of Native Americans with a unique practice for training young braves. On the night of a boy's thirteenth birthday, he was placed in a dense forest to spend the entire night alone. Before that night, he had never been away from the security of his family and tribe. One particular young man was blindfolded and led many miles into the wilderness. He was instructed not to remove the blindfold for an hour. On this particular night, dark clouds obscured the moon and stars, and when he removed the blindfold all he could see was utter darkness. Every time a twig snapped, he visualised a wild animal ready to pounce. Every time an animal howled, he imagined a wolf leaping out of the darkness. He spent a terrifying night on the edge of panic, but he didn't leave. After what seemed like an eternity, the first rays of sunlight began to lighten the eastern sky. Looking around, the boy saw flowers, trees, and the outline of the path. Then, to his utter astonishment, he beheld the figure of a man standing just a few feet away, armed with a long bow and arrow. It was the boy's father. He had been there all night long.

You know, you may not "feel" His presence all the time but He is there. He said, "I will never leave you nor forsake you," And He does care. The Bible says, we can "Cast all our cares upon Him, for He cares for you."

Third: You don't have to be afraid because God knows everything about you—and He still loves you.

Jesus has some revolutionary truth about how much God cares for you as an individual. He says every hair on your head has been numbered - and He knows the number. As I was taking a shower, God might have thought, "Well, there goes hair number 4,567 down the drain." I didn't even notice it, but He did. That means God is concerned with even the tiny details of your life you don't even think about. Now I want to ask a question and anyone except a bald man may answer it: "How many hairs are on your head?" Experts tell us if you are blonde (a real blonde) you have around 145,000 hairs; if you are a redhead you only have 90,000; and if you have black or brown hair, you have around 120,000 hairs. I'm amazed someone took the time to count! The point is, God knows things about you even you don't know. In other words, God knows you better than you know yourself!

The Psalmist declares: "Oh Lord, you have searched me and you know me. You know when I sit and when I rise; you perceive my thoughts from afar... How precious to me are your thoughts, O God! How vast is the sum of them! Were I to count them, they would outnumber the grains of sand." Amazing! Not only does God count your hairs, He thinks about you so many times each day, the number exceeds the grains of sand on the beach. When I'm by the sea I love to walk on the beach, but I try to brush off all the sand before I get back into the car. As I'm brushing off the sand, I can think, "There's another thought, there's another thought. Thank you God for thinking of me!"

Not only are you more valuable than many sparrows to God, He is interested in every area of life. You may wonder how the Creator of the universe has time to think about you? That's just it. He isn't bound by time. A day is like a thousand years, and a second is the same as a century with Him. God can run the entire universe, while at the same time watching over a sparrow or listening to your prayer or thinking about you as if you were the only creature in His creation. It's like the sun in the sky. Our mighty sun keeps the planets in orbit, but it will also ripen the tomatoes in your garden as if it had nothing else to do. That's why you don't have to be afraid–because God knows you. He knows your fears and He knows your needs. He knows you better than you know yourself - and yet He still loves you!

There is a great verse on fear, "There is no fear in love. But perfect love drives out fear" (1 John 4:18). You know, for a long time I struggled with that verse, because I thought the "perfect love" was the kind of love I should have for God. I figured the reason I could be afraid was because I didn't have a perfect love for God. One day, God showed me the "perfect love" was the love He has for me! That made all the difference! Even though God knows every time I have failed Him in the past and every time I will fail Him in the future; He still maintains a perfect love for me - so I don't have to be afraid!

Fourth: You don't have to be afraid because God wants to have a personal relationship with you for eternity.

The camera shots made during and after a terrorist attack have been played over and over again. Many are from mobile phones. Usually the sound track is muted, but sometimes you are able to hear what the camera operator or the bystanders are saying. The single cry heard time and time again was, "Oh, God!" or "Oh, my God!" Think about it. There is a basic need and a basic impulse deep within the soul of every person that cries out to connect with God during the most traumatic times of life. People crying out to God or falling on their knees to pray just reveals this basic urge. God made you with a hole in your soul that could only be filled with a relationship with Him. People spend their entire lives trying to fill the emptiness with possessions, pleasure, power or prestige. But it's like trying to force the square peg in the round hole. The hole in your heart is shaped like a cross and only Jesus can fill it.

You may wonder, "How can I face the future without fear? I don't know what's going to happen!" Take a moment and think about the word *"LIFE"*. Circle in your mind the two middle letters. Life is full of *"ifs."* There is so much uncertainty. Derek, what are we going to do IF there is war? What are we going to do IF there are more attacks on our streets? What are we going to do IF our economy takes a further nosedive? *If, If, If.*

My response is we need to do the same thing we would do *if* none of those things happen. We need to completely place our lives in God's hands. We must keep on trusting God and work on developing an intimate relationship with Him. If you take the remaining two letters of *LIFE* and remove the "if," it's a reminder of *Life Eternal.* There is this L for *LIFE* and then there is E for *ETERNITY.* Our existence doesn't end with the death of our body, because we also have an eternal soul. But we can still face the future without fear because Jesus has made a way for us to know Him and to live with Him forever, even after this old body dies. We don't have to be afraid of what may happen over the next few months and you don't have to be afraid about where you will spend eternity. A real Christian doesn't fear when confronted with death or eternity.

John Wesley, founder of Methodism, was baptised as an infant and confirmed in the Anglican Church. He went through all the rituals of the church and considered himself a good Christian. He was so good in fact; he travelled across the Atlantic to serve as a missionary in the colonies of Georgia and the Carolinas. The entire time, however, he knew deep inside his heart that although he was very religious, there was something missing. He had very little success and, feeling like a failure, he boarded a ship to return to England. On the return voyage he met a group of Moravian Christians who were vibrant and joyous in their faith, and it intrigued Wesley. One night the ship encountered a ferocious storm. It ripped the sails and tossed the little ship for hours. Everyone, including the crew, thought they would sink and drown. Being on a little wooden ship in the middle of the Atlantic in the middle of the storm must be the closest thing to being on a doomed airliner today. Wesley was literally trembling from fright. When he glanced at the Moravians he saw to his surprise they were smiling and calmly singing songs of praise. In that one moment, he realised he was not saved. He did not have the kind of inner peace that could sustain him when he confronted death. After the storm passed (as all storms do), he wrote about the Moravians, "the wilder the waves, the calmer they sang." His fear convinced him that his heart had never been changed by Christ.

He wrote: "I went to America to convert the Indians, but, oh, who shall convert me? I have a fair summer religion. I can talk well: nay and believe myself while no danger is near; but let death look me in the face and my spirit is troubled. Neither can I say, 'for me to die is gain'. Oh, who shall deliver me from this fear of death?"

Upon returning to England, Wesley attended a meeting on Aldersgate Street. It was May 24, 1738. While a minister was reading from Luther's preface to Romans, Wesley later wrote, "I felt my heart strangely warmed. I felt I did trust Christ, Christ alone for salvation; and an assurance was given me that He had taken away my sins, even mine!" After meeting Christ, his life was totally transformed. And there are thousands of Methodist churches, which stand as a testimony of a man who learned it takes a personal relationship with God to enable a person to face eternity without fear.

Will you trust Christ today with your life and with your eternity? If you will, you don't have to fear death or the grave. That's how you can face the future without fear!

Practical insights about fear.

There is a *healthy fear*. You teach a child to not play with matches and to take care when crossing a road. The apostle Paul wrote, "Work out your salvation with fear and trembling." There is a healthy fear of not getting the best out of our Christian life.

It is *unhealthy fear* we need to confront. We begin life as babies with a fear of loud noises. We grow as children fearing the darkness or falling. We reach adolescence with a load of fears imposed by life events. We catch the infection of imagined fears of what might happen.

What makes you afraid? Is it the unknown? The untried? Ill-health? Too old to be useful? Rejection? Money problems? The one thing we all have in common is fear. Education consists in being afraid at the right time. Our emotional conditioning makes us afraid most of the time. Keeping in mind what Jesus says, here are the basic steps for dealing with your fears.

Describe your fear.
Single them out one by one: "My fears are the following." Look them in the face. Is my fear based in a person or situation? Is it real or imagined?

Displace your fear.
Why will a woman run into a burning building when she is rightly afraid of fire? Because her baby is in that building. The greater love displaces the fear of the flames. The same emotions that channel fear channel love. Tell yourself God's truth about yourself. "God really does love me. He will help me."

Dare your fear.
Fear can become a habit. Make a choice to confront what you fear and do the thing God would want. His Spirit is with you to help.

It's been well said, "366 times the bible says "do not be afraid". That's one for every day and an extra one for leap year.

Printed in the United Kingdom
by Lightning Source UK Ltd.
119557UK00001B/127-198